# Nantucket Summers

# The Story of a Family and a Very Special Cottage Called Sunnycliffe

## Katharine Stanley-Brown Abbott

*Katharine Stanley-Brown Abbott*

*Pinniped Press*
*Ipswich, Massachusetts*

Cover: Sunnycliffe c. 1888 *from Nantucket Historical Association*
Back cover: Sankaty Light

Nantucket Summers:  The Story of a Family and a Very Special
Cottage Called Sunnycliffe
© 1996 Katharine Stanley-Brown Abbott

ISBN  0-9651777-0-X

Manufactured in the United States of America
by Journeyman Press, Inc.
Newburyport, Massachusetts  01950

and published by
Pinniped Press
PO Box 148
Ipswich, Massachusetts  01938


Printed on Recycled Paper

# Table of Contents

# Acknowledgements

The genesis of this book came as I was taking a writing course at Radcliffe taught by the late Martin Robbins. He encouraged me to start, to work hard and not to settle for anything less than the best. His criticisms were always honest, fair and thoughtful. Through Martin I learned the joy of rewriting. I wish he had been here as my guide and friend as I wrote, rewrote, edited and completed the manuscript.

Without the advice, guidance and technical skills of Jonathan Labaree, *Nantucket Summers* would never have found its way to print. He has acted as typesetter, designer and, finally, as publisher, for all of which I am most grateful.

Others have been supportive and helpful as well. They include my brother and sister-in-law, Ted and Jeanne Stanley-Brown, my cousin Katrina Debevoise, my four children and my husband Gordon.

My greatest thanks go to Gordon Abbott who has urged me on, offered professional help along the way, read and reread the manuscript. In editing the final copy, he cleverly brought the book to life while maintaining the integrity of my writing style. He is my best friend and most fair-minded critic.

# *Foreword*

I found my mother's autobiography, hand-written in pencil in a
six-by-nine inch notebook eight years after she died in 1972.
Why I hadn't noticed it before then is a mystery, but its arrival
at that point in time was auspicious. I was taking writing
courses at Radcliffe that involved reaching back into my past.
Anyone who has taken similar courses, or even filled out a college or graduate school application, has been asked the same
questions. "Describe a significant incident in your past that has
affected the present" or "What is your most important memory
of your childhood". That kind of thing.

At the same time, with four children grown up, I had an
embryonic interest in my own past, curiosity about my ancestors and an emerging urge to make the children aware of their
heritage.

Then there was Nantucket where I had spent 25 consecutive
summers in the house that my grandfather had built in 1887,
and that my brother and I sold in 1976.

Gradually, I saw how this book might develop. As I read
my mother's story, written when she was 78 and 79, I found a
wealth of family history and personal reflection, many delightful anecdotes that brought family members alive, and, not sur-
prisingly, some inaccuracies, especially with dates. But, then I
discovered some wonderful source material: my grandmother's diaries from 1884-1888 as well as six of her barely legible
travel diaries. Most fascinating, however, were the many boxes
of letters from my mother and father to each other over 20 summers when she was in Nantucket and he in Cleveland and then
Washington. Sometimes they each wrote the other twice a day,
detailing all their thoughts and activities. The ones from my
mother, in particular, fill out a picture of life in Sconset during
the 1920's and 1930's that would be hard to duplicate.

As I wove my mental tapestry, I realized that the memories I had of my childhood were sometimes the same, and sometimes quite different from what my mother's letters and biography told me. So, too, were my grandmother's, father's and brother's memories different. For this book, I have used primarily the voices of women; my grandmother, my mother and myself.

It's hard to know if this is a story about a family, a house, or a place. Since the family lived in the house on Nantucket Island, it is really an interwoven story of all three elements. The Olivers, Henrys and Stanley-Browns aren't remarkable people. Nor are they celebrities, distinguished citizens or folk heroes. Rather, they are typical of a certain group of Americans who enjoyed a life style that no longer exists. They came from honest stock with solid virtues and values. And, in a modest way, they were pioneers when they made their way to a flat, windswept island off the Massachusetts coast in 1887 to build a summer cottage. Their stories reveal hope, happiness, virtue and satisfaction. They also reveal regret, sadness, disappointment, and compliance. And, aren't these similar to the emotions of most families, in one form or another?

I hope that this book contains something for many people. For those who are interested in place, here's a glimpse of Nantucket as it used to be. For social historians, it is a story of a family caught in time, whose actions reflect the mores of an era. And for my family, it's a look at part of your heritage. For me it has been a wonderful experience to weave together the strands of family history and recall the Nantucket of my youth.

# Nantucket Summers

# *Chapter One*

## *The Gift*

Dr. Charles Oliver pushed through the swinging glass doors and hurried down the long corridor of Old Blakely until he reached the room where his young patient was recovering from cataract surgery. Although only 34 himself, Dr. Oliver was a respected member of the staff at Philadelphia's Wills Eye Hospital and was considered a brilliant surgeon by his colleagues. This particular morning in 1887, he was pleased that the rather new surgical procedure had gone so well.

*Charles Augustus Oliver, M.D.*

The young man, still in bed, appeared nervous and, with some hesitation, confessed that he couldn't pay his bill. "I can, however," he added quickly, "give you two lots and beach rights, Dr. Oliver, on a sandspit in the Atlantic called Nantucket."

"What in the world would I do with that?" asked Charles.

"If I kept the land myself," his patient replied, "I would build a hunting lodge."

Charles tried to imagine how he might use the property, and finally said with a smile, "Well, I've never heard of the place, but if that's all I'm going to get, I'll take it!"

Having a scholarly turn of mind, Charles Oliver decided to learn something about the small island, six miles wide and 14 miles long, known as Nantucket which lay 30 miles off the mainland of Massachusetts. An Indian myth told how long before white men settled on the island, "red whalers" had fished the waters south of Cape Cod. A mighty giant liked to sleep on the warm, soft sands of the Cape. One restless night he kicked his feet around. The next morning he was annoyed to find sand in his moccasins. Taking them off, he flung the contents as far as he could across the sea, thus, legend has it, creating Martha's Vineyard, Nantucket and the sandy shoals around them.

The story amused Charles, but the scientific explanation interested him more. Nantucket, he learned, was part of the terminal moraine caused by the last North American glacier. Warmed by the Gulf Stream, which passes two hundred miles south of the Island on its way northeast to Ireland, the glacier began to melt. As tons of debris-loaded ice moved eastward, water levels rose along the coastal plain, and the land that wasn't drowned by the sea became Nantucket, Martha's Vineyard and Cape Cod. The converging Gulf Stream and cold Atlantic waters bring hurricanes from the tropics and northeast storms from Nova Scotia that sweep over the Island, shroud it with fog during the summer, and fill the harbor with ice in winter. But the Gulf Stream also produces a benign climate that supports profuse vegetation, both southern and northern. Bearberry, golden heather, holly, arbutus, sweet fern, azalea, elderberry, wild rose, pitch pine and prickly pear enjoy each other's company. Another Island phenomenon is the coarse Sankaty Sand, made up of mineral fragments of quartz, clay, iron oxide, green glauconite and garnet which give it irregular streaks of color — brown, red, yellow, gray and white.

That spring, packing his portmanteau, Charles Oliver went to see his land. He took the train from Philadelphia to New York, sailed on the overnight steamer up Long Island Sound, and arrived at Fall River the following morning. After a quick breakfast, he boarded the first of two trains, changing at the little town of Myricks, for the two-hour trip to New Bedford. Today, he would have made the journey by car in 30 minutes. The last leg of the voyage was made aboard the paddle wheel steamer *Nantucket*, flagship of the recently-formed New Bedford, Martha's Vineyard and Nantucket Steamship Company. As she churned her way across Nantucket Sound, she passed Cross Rip lightship close aboard, halfway point of the trip. Passengers often tossed well-tied newspapers and magazines over the side for the lightship crew to fish out of the water with nets attached to long poles. The soggy offerings were accepted gratefully, for crew members had little other contact with civilization for long weeks at a time.

Exhausted after his journey, Charles spent the night in a rooming house in "Town," as the natives called the settlement of Nantucket. The next day, in a hired horse-drawn carriage, he drove the nine, dusty miles of dirt road across the moors to Siasconset, an unpretentious fishing village. There, on a high bluff facing eastward, one hundred feet above a long, empty sweep of Sankaty sand and breaking surf, was his land. On this dramatic headland of an otherwise flat island, there were no trees, but lots of sweet fern, wild roses and bayberry bushes. A rutted road ran the length of the Bluff from sturdy, red-banded Sankaty light house, built in 1850, down to the little village with its low, gray-shingled fishermen's houses clustered near the community water pump. A few summer cottages stood between the lighthouse and village.

"Does the wind always blow like this?" Charles asked his driver.

"It does, and that's what keeps the Island nice and cool in July and August," was the reply "...don't usually have heat waves out here."

Charles thought about the stifling summers in Philadelphia and decided then and there to construct a summer cottage.

"Tell me," he said to his driver, "who would be the best builder in Town?"

"Why, that's easy, it's George Gibbs."

A former ship's carpenter, Gibbs was used to providing exacting joiner work, plus he was said to be thoroughly honest and reliable. Charles approved his selection immediately.

"I'm to be married next June, Mr. Gibbs.," he said. "Do you think you could build me a nice cottage by then. Nothing fancy, mind you, but solid and cozy."

"Of course, Dr. Oliver. I'll build you a fine house that will last you a hundred years or more."

Satisfied, Charles deposited $10,000 in the Pacific National Bank in Town for Mr. Gibbs to draw upon until the house was complete. He then returned to Philadelphia and wrote a long letter to share the news with his fiancée, Mary Henry of South Orange, New Jersey. What better wedding present could he give her than a summer cottage on a lovely island off the New England coast?

# Chapter Two

# The Attraction

*Mary Schermerhorn Henry (right) with her best friend, Theo Connet, 1887*

Mary Henry and Charles Oliver had such different personalities that it is remarkable they met, fell in love and married. A mutual friend brought the two together in Montrose, New York in September of 1886. Mary was 25 years old. Charles was 33.

Mary's family had roots in Germany and Holland. Her father, Lewis B. Henry, traced his ancestry to Hanover, Germany where his grandfather, John Phillips Henry, was born in 1741. The Henrys moved to Bristol, England and eventually to New York City, where John Henry opened a clothing store. His son, Philip, born in 1786, was a draper and tailor. The brothers and sons of these early Henrys were honorable citizens who fought for their country, joined the Masons, had their own church pews, and played leading role with civic organizations.

Lewis B. Henry was the second youngest of Philip and Mary Ann Henry's 10 children. He and his four brothers all worked in the drygoods and importing firm of Henry, Smith & Townsend, the second largest establishment of its kind in the country. Unfortunately, the firm failed shortly after the Civil War began. Accounts in the South alone owed the company more than a million dollars. But Lewis B. Henry honorably paid all creditors out of his own pocket at the expense of his wife's horse and carriage. To save money, he also moved his family out of New York City to South Orange, New Jersey where he owned a summer cottage.

Lewis was a canny business man and realized that beet from the North, not cane from the South, would be an important source of sugar after the Civil War. To this end, he formed a sugar brokerage firm that soon flourished and was carried on by two of his sons well into this century. The commute from South Orange to New York proved to be long and tiresome, so Lewis, his obligations met, moved his family to a four-story house in East Orange that had been built for Lucretia Mott, the nineteenth century suffragist. Still country, the Henry's land included a large barn, an apple orchard and a tiny brook. Lewis died in 1892, but the house was occupied by Henry descendants until the late 1950's. When it was sold, it was a charming relic of another era, surrounded by high-rise buildings in the middle of what was by then a thriving suburban community.

Mary's mother, Catherine Elvenah was born in Homer, New York, near the city of Rochester. She was the second of six children of Jacob Maus Schermerhorn and Louisa Anna Barber. The Schermerhorns, whose name was taken from the two towns of Schermer and Hoorn that flank the Hoorn River, fourteen miles north of Amsterdam, arrived in Niew Amsterdam in 1622. While some family members remained in New York to amass their fortune, Jacob Maus' ancestors moved to communities in upstate New York which must have seemed more like the Dutch towns they had known. With them these Schermerhorns brought solid virtues. They were hard-working, dutiful, religious and thrifty. The men served as officers in the militia, one was a justice of the peace, another mayor of Albany. Catherine's father, Jacob Maus, practiced law in Rochester. He was a graduate of Union College and eventually, with his brother Abraham, founded the Bank of Monroe in Rochester, and became president of the Syracuse & Binghamton Railroad, which he helped to build.

Above all, the Schermerhorns were practical and expeditious. In 1829 the courtship of Jacob Maus Schermerhorn and Louisa Barber was well under way. Louisa lived her whole life in upstate Homer, where her father Jedediah was a successful merchant and principal of the local school. When Jacob Maus had decided to ask Mr. Barber for Louisa's hand in marriage, he took a stagecoach from Rochester, quite unaware that his traveling companion, Andrew D. White, later the President of Cornell University, was on an identical mission. Both young men, equally handsome and eligible, stepped out of the coach in Homer. Jacob set out immediately for the Barber house, a few blocks away. Andrew White, however, went to the tavern, washed his hands and face, changed out of his dusty clothes, and then walked over to the Barber house where old Hannah opened the door and led him into the parlor. Mr. and Mrs. Barber were seated with Louisa and Jacob Schermerhorn nearby. Taking Mr. Barber aside, Andrew White professed his love for Louisa and asked for her hand. "Dear me," Jedediah said, "I gave her away to Mr. Schermerhorn not five minutes ago!"

Jacob Maus
Schermerhorn, 1882

Louisa Barbor Schermerhorn in a portrait by C.W. Jarvis, second son of portraitist J.W. Jarvis

*Catherine Schermerhorn
Henry circa 1865*

Louisa and Jacob lived a long and happy life together, first in Rochester where their seven children were born, and then at "The Hedges" in Homer. When their daughter Catherine married Lewis B. Henry in 1856, the newlyweds moved to New York City where six of their eight children were born. Louisa, the eldest arrived in 1857; Mary, my grandmother, was ushered in with the Civil War in 1861; Edward was born in 1863, Alice in 1866, Katharine in 1868, and Lewis in 1872. The youngest two, Anna (1875) and Jacob (1876) were both born in South Orange.

The Henrys were happy, jolly and religious. Strong family bonds were forged by the solid and serene devotion of the two parents who expected their children to be honest, loyal, respectful, and to adhere to rules and traditions their ancestors had observed for centuries. For the Henry children, life was predictable and pleasant and they seldom questioned it. Much was given to them and much was expected. "Duty Before Pleasure" is a family motto which was carried through the generations.

Until her marriage to Charles Oliver, my grandmother Mary Henry lived with her family in East Orange. She had strawberry blonde hair, intense blue eyes, a quick wit, and equally quick temper. She was romantic, impetuous, unpredictable, and loved beauty in all its forms. She embraced life's emotions with the intensity of grand opera — thrilling moments

*The Hedges
Homer, New York*

of happiness, plunges to the depths of tragedy, wrongs to be righted, sadness and pain to be endured. And when her visions of life failed to coincide with reality, she was devastated. She empathized with the heroines of Sir Walter Scott's novels as well as with the Victorian poets that she loved. At parades, her hand was on her heart. The Bible was her daily companion. Of education, she had little but quite enough for her day. She attended Miss Mankin's and Dearborn Morgan School in Orange until the age of sixteen. From then on she had private singing lessons and, with her sisters Alice and Katharine, she studied French and embroidery. Many days were devoted to sewing under the expert eye of Clara, the seamstress who came to the house twice a week. Mary often did the family marketing and a bit of cooking, and she helped her mother run the household; all activities considered suitable preparations for marriage. She also spent a few hours each morning teaching her little brother and sister to read and write.

*Nicholas B. Oliver (1740—1840). Father of William George Oliver, Grandfather of George Powell Oliver, Great-grandfather of Charles Augustus Oliver*

Religion played an important role in the Henrys' life. Every morning before breakfast family members and servants attended prayer service in the parlor. Most of every Sunday was given over to church — Sunday school, Sunday service, afternoon service or Vespers, and hymn-singing in the evening.

On weekdays, Mary wrote letters to her family and friends, a habit she continued all her life. She spent long hours talking with her mother or sisters in the age before the telephone was invented. And she and her female friends visited back and forth. It was an easy trolley ride to South Orange where most of them lived. Pretty and vivacious, Mary had lots of suitors who arranged tennis games, carriage rides, and dances; and in the winter, sleigh rides, skating and coasting parties. With a vanity of which her Dutch ancestors might not have approved, Mary loved to dress up and show off her dainty figure and tiny waist. Her conversation was witty and lively, and she enjoyed the attention of many suitors. She was particularly fond of a group of Yale classmates, including Prescott Bush, grandfather of President George Bush.

*Major William George Oliver (1779—1824). Grandfather of Katharine Oliver Stanley-Brown*

Charles Oliver had a very different background, but one that appeared fascinating and exotic to country-bred Mary Henry. At twenty-six, Charles' father George, a physician in Philadelphia, had married the beautiful twenty-five year old daughter of José Nicolas Suarez of Ferrol, Spain. Don José was active in shipping and overseas trade with Cuba and the Argentine, having left Spain with his wife Caroline and moved to Philadelphia, where business prospects seemed more promis-

*Major Surgeon General George Powell Oliver (1824—1884) in 1862*

ing. Their only child, Marie Louisa, was born in June, 1825. Alone in a foreign country, with her own family now far away, Caroline was shattered, nine years later, when Don José was drowned in a shipwreck leaving her a widow with a small daughter. She was, however, also left with a comfortable inheritance which insured Marie Louisa's education for two years at St. Peter's Convent, followed by private lessons at home. In the limited social circle of mid-Nineteenth century Philadelphia, Marie Louisa met George Oliver. They fell in love and were married when she was just twenty-one years old.

Their only child was Charles Augustus Oliver, born in Cincinnati, Ohio in 1853, where his father George spent three years as the city physician. The Olivers returned to Philadelphia and Charles attended Central High School, received an M.A. from Lafayette College, and was graduated from the University of Pennsylvania Medical School in 1876. Like his father, Charles showed an early passion for medicine, a passion that would consume much of his life and a great part of his personality.

Although not large in stature, Charles Oliver was an impressive figure. His oval face, high forehead and deep-set blue eyes were like his father's. He had his Spanish mother's olive skin. His black hair began to recede before he reached thirty, and with a trimmed moustache, steel-rimmed glasses and formal three-piece suits, a stiff collar and bow tie, he looked older than his years. His mien was serious and reserved, and his approach to life scholarly. When not working long hours at the hospital, he plunged into research on eye disease that led, eventually, to a two-volume textbook on the subject, written with his good friend, Dr. George Norris. As his reputation grew, Charles was called upon to lecture in Philadelphia and abroad. His books were published in several languages, and he devoted time he hardly had to help establish eye clinics for indigent patients.

Given such different personalities, it's little wonder that the courtship of Charles and Mary was long and uneven. Charles was initially charmed with Mary's vivacity and wit, so different from his own reticence and sense of privacy. Mary, for her part, was flattered to have captured the interest of a distinguished scholar. Gradually, as they came to know each other, they discovered a mutual love of music, and the pleasure of outdoor activities. Charles enjoyed the informality of Mary's large and jolly family, for his life before he met the Henrys was, without siblings, a lonely one. A real impediment, however, was a difference in religion. The Henrys were devout Episcopalians and

Charles, through his mother, was Catholic. Until Charles agreed to be married in Mary's church the Henrys were anxious, but once that hurdle was past, the subject was never mentioned again.

Mary fretted about the relationship. Not given to intellectual analysis, she wondered whether her life with Charles would match those of her heroes and heroines in fiction. She translated her dreams into real expectations. Did Charles measure up? He did his best, leaving Philadelphia late Saturday after a full day at the hospital, to spend the night and Sunday in Orange. He and Mary went to church and he loved to hear her clear, sweet voice singing the hymns. At times they walked in Llewellyn Park before Sunday lunch, but there were few moments to be alone. Mary's brothers and sisters were usually at home. Charles had numerous medical meetings, and upon his return he was often tired. From Mary's diary it's clear that she and Charles spent hours talking and trying to understand each other. When he could, Charles stayed through Sunday night and Mary fixed him breakfast Monday morning, often picking him a bouquet of fresh flowers. On Valentine's Day in 1887, Mary wrote in her diary: "Went to the mail this morning, found a sweet note from CAO, telling, I thought, of flowers to come. Found out my mistake." Instead of flowers and a love note, Charles had sent "old family papers" and medical tracts to read.

But, on March 27 she wrote: "A most beautiful day. Stayed in bed until eleven; then dressed and waited for Dr. O in the parlor before the fire. He came an hour late, talked all the afternoon, then CAO had a little talk with Papa and my *fate was sealed*."

In mid-April, Mary went to Philadelphia to meet Charles's mother, Marie Louisa Suarez Oliver, and wrote of the visit: "A queer day, hopes, fear, doubts and pleasures." When it was over she felt sad and unhappy. Marie Louisa could have written the same thing. She faced sharing her only son with a pretty, but perhaps too frivolous young woman of a different background and religion. Philadelphia seemed stiff and formal to Mary and, for the first time, she saw how dedicated Charles was to his profession. What she did not see in the misty world of young love, was the impact this dedication would have on her marriage. During her visit, Charles took Mary, not to art museums and concert halls, but to his office, the Wills Eye Hospital and the Insane Women's Department of the Norristown Hospital.

Yet when Charles and Mary visited her grandparents in Homer, they canned peaches together and put up raspberry vinegar with Mary's sister Katie. They played tennis, rowed on the river near Homer and took pleasant carriage rides. Mary's Uncle Maus Schermerhorn discussed the family furniture they might have for the house at 1507 Locust Street that Charles had bought. As the fall progressed, Mary hemstitched linens and sent them, along with pillows, to Philadelphia. She chose wall paper from samples that Charles had given her. And with Clara's help, she sewed her trousseau: a dressing sacque, dresses, skirts, blouses and suits. Gradually the nest was feathered.

On June 6, 1888, Bishop Huntington joined Mary and Charles in holy matrimony at Grace Church in Orange. Mary wore white tulle, Marie Louisa Oliver's white silk lace mantilla, and carried a bouquet of orange blossoms, stephanotis and white roses. Her three sisters and two best friends were bridesmaids. George Norris was best man. After a reception and wedding breakfast at the Henry house, the newly-weds left for a three months' wedding trip to Europe. If Mary was distressed that Charles interrupted their honeymoon with medical meetings in Munich, Vienna and Dresden, she would remember the happy work-free weeks they had in Paris and in London. By the time they returned home in September, Mary was pregnant.

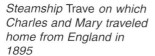

*Steamship* Trave *on which Charles and Mary traveled home from England in 1895*

# Chapter Three
## The Henry Women

Catherine Henry, matriarch of the family, was a quiet source of strength and faith. From portraits and family photographs, she looks serene and gentle. Her thick dark hair, never cut, hung down to her knees. She wore it parted in the middle, then parted again on either side of the middle at the crown, looping it into a large bun at the back. At 80, she had never had a filling in her white teeth. My mother remembered that her grandmother gazed at the great double mahogany bed where all her children had been born and said: "You know, I have never made a bed in my life. I think I should learn now." With instructions from her astounded and timid little chambermaid Elizabeth, Catherine then made her first bed. Of course, life was easy with the help of many Elizabeths to smooth the way.

*Catherine Henry in her 70s*

Catherine had firm ideas on morals and behavior which she passed on to her family. Again, my mother recalled an evening — she was about 16 — when an awkward and very nervous young man came to call on her and left on his rubbers. When he departed, Catherine took her granddaughter's hand in hers and said: "That young man who came to see you tonight had no manners. Remember when you marry, if you do not find a Philadelphian who will ask you to do so, someone from Baltimore might be all right, or as a last resort, Boston. But never consider a young man from New York or the West. You will not find any gentlemen there." Had Catherine Henry forgotten that her own husband came from New York?

After Lewis B. Henry died in 1892, Catherine, newly widowed, spent part of each summer with Mary at Sunnycliffe. In a long black dress and ruffled, voile cap, she sat on the straight-backed wooden bench at the edge of the Bluff, looking out at the endless stretch of ocean, perfectly calm and content. Her marriage had been happy, she could be proud of all her children who were dutiful, God-fearing, hard-working and virtuous, and she was at peace with her world. That her world was limited and that she had been sheltered from the harsher side of

The Henrys in East Orange—1890

Catherine Henry in black. Mary Henry Oliver holds her hand. To her left are her daughters Alice Henry Carter with John Franklin Carter, Jr. To her right, Katharine Schermerhorn Henry (Mrs. Robert Storer Stephenson). On her right, Louisa Schermerhorn Henry holding Sarah Swift Carter

Standing in back, Robert Storer Stephenson, John Franklin Carter and Charles Augustus Oliver holding Henry Carter. Leaning against sickle pear tree, Lewis Chauncey Henry with Norris Schermerhorn Oliver. Seated, Jacob Schermerhorn Henry with "Laddie", Katharine Schermerhorn Oliver and Edward Schermerhorn Henry it, did not concern or unsettle her. Misfortune was met with equanimity, inner wisdom and a strong faith in God's power and will.

Louisa Henry, born in 1857, was her eldest daughter. Like all Henrys, she had a high forehead, small mouth, straight nose and blue eyes set near together. As she grew, she became the tallest girl in the family, and possessed a certain serene, statuesque quality that, in adulthood, gave her a formidable and elegant presence. What she might have accomplished is conjecture for at eighteen she was sent to live with her invalid grandmother, Louisa Schermerhorn. A less dutiful girl might have rebelled at such a predetermined fate, but Louisa never questioned her parents' order and remained her grandmother's companion for 23 years.

Louisa Schermerhorn, Jacob Maus Schermerhorn's widow, had a medical condition referred to by the family in hushed tones as "the flow." Undoubtedly this was a menstrual dysfunction that would have been cured today with simple surgery. But in the 1870's, Louisa's doctor prescribed only complete bed rest, except for one hour a day. So for 18 years, Louisa Schermerhorn managed the staff of "The Hedges" from her canopied, four-poster bed.

At the end of a quiet, elm-shaded lane, "The Hedges" had spacious rooms, heavy Victorian furniture, dark wood walls and floor, and wide porches. Paris Barber, Louisa Schermerhorn's brother, was a landscape architect before the title had been adopted by the profession. He designed four identical square gardens, divided from one another by hedges of arborvitae (hence the house's name) that led down the slope of land to the little Tioughnioga River. One garden contained beautiful standard roses. A second held flowers for picking. A third provided fresh vegetables for the table. And the fourth garden was home to a variety of herbs. The arbor off the dining room drooped with huge Hamburg grapes in the summer. On warm afternoons, in the shade of a tall umbrella tree, the Schermerhorns had their tea on gold and white Dresden china from a table that was wheeled across the perfectly trimmed lawn. Old Hannah made sure there were rolled cucumber or watercress sandwiches and a plate of lace or sand cookies. Jacob Schermerhorn, hot and tired from his day at the bank, refreshed himself with a glass of Port.

For young Louisa Henry, the days were long and boring. There were few people her age to meet in tiny Homer, only an endless routine of meals, practice on the old square piano in the parlor and attending to her grandmother's needs. This included reading aloud, writing letters and learning to hemstitch linen. Louisa Schermerhorn, however, was keen of mind and, at the age of 80, engaged a local schoolmaster to teach her Greek as she wanted to read the *Iliad* in the original. But for young Louisa Henry, time lay heavy and what she dreaded most were the afternoon outings. Every day at four o'clock, her grandmother, dressed by her Scottish nurse, Lana, walked down the wide staircase and out the front door where the horses waited under the porte-cochère. She stepped into the barouche and with Louisa Henry at her side, drove through town. The windows were closed and curtained to prevent a chill and keep out sunshine. Occasionally, they stopped to give clothing or food to those less fortunate. The high point of Louisa Henry's day, she told my mother years later, were the moments when the gardener brought fresh flowers in for her to arrange.

Once, however, she visited her Aunt Anna and Uncle John Fisher in Philadelphia, and by happy chance met a Mr. Tunis. In a short time the love-starved young girl found true happiness and Mr. Tunis proposed marriage. Although he was not of the same social station as Louisa, which in those days was a crucial feature of a "suitable" union, Louisa's mother and father gave the couple their blessing. But, when they went to Homer to meet Louisa Schermerhorn, she refused her consent and sent Mr. Tunis packing. Since Louisa Henry had made herself indispensable to her grandmother, her leaving was unthinkable. With her usual fortitude, Louisa accepted her grandmother's decision, and curiously, seemed not to regret it. Or perhaps, over time, she came to rationalize what she could not change.

*The Henry Girls; Left to right: Alice Carter, Mary Oliver, and Louisa Henry, 1912*

"When I see what problems my sisters and brothers had with marriage," she told a young nephew, "I was glad to have avoided it."

As a reward for her selfless care, although it must have been somewhat too little and too late, Louisa Schermerhorn, upon her death, left her granddaughter all her possessions and a small inheritance. Louisa immediately moved to Boston and spent her summers, not with her family, but in what she hoped was a more lively setting, the Hackmatack Inn at Halifax, Nova Scotia. There she died at the age of 77. Perhaps one reason for her absence from Nantucket was that she and Mary had very different temperaments. They adored each other and hated to be apart, but were miserable and got on each other's nerves when they were together. Mary was high-spirited and self-centered. Louisa was quiet and unselfish, happy in her later years to smooth over family differences by letter and to help her nephews and nieces.

Mary was five years old when her sister Alice Schermerhorn Henry was born. Alice was petite and well-proportioned, but as she grew up her face lacked the gentle softness of the other Henry girls. Her features were set wider apart and were more angular. She had a gentle wit and was fun-loving and lively. Of all the girls, she was best attuned to domesticity. It was just as well as in 1890, she married John Franklin Carter, an Episcopal minister and was eventually the mother of three sets of twin boys and one girl, all of whom she brought up mostly by herself!

John Carter came to religion oddly. He attended Columbia School of Mines where he studied to be an engineer. The end of the nineteenth century, however, saw a change in religious perceptions. Fire and brimstone gave way to a more reasoned and human approach. Guided by two forward-looking New England theologians, Phillips Brooks and Bishop William Lawrence, church schools sprang up, spreading the thesis that privilege had its obligations. Young men were encouraged to make the world a better place to live. A clergyman was not only a Sunday purveyor of the Gospel; he was a flesh and blood human being as well. John Carter soon realized that digging for souls might be more rewarding than digging for minerals and he promptly enrolled at Cambridge Theological Seminary. Upon graduation, he accepted curateships in New York and Fall River, eventually settling in Williamstown, Massachusetts, where he was appointed Rector of St. John's Episcopal Church. It was the perfect place for a large family to live, and it gave

John Carter a chance to enjoy his favorite activities: boxing, mountain-climbing and brisk walking.

In addition to bringing up seven lively children, Alice Carter involved herself actively in the life of Williamstown. On Sunday evenings she encouraged Williams College students to join her family for supper and games. Alice was proud of her Sunday night chafing-dish suppers, although her repertoire was limited to three dishes: Welsh Rarebit, Lobster Newburgh and Scrambled Eggs with cocoa. If Alice was a frugal housekeeper, she was, as one of her sons said, "a bit casual about money, always had trouble with her checkbook and accounts, and used her own microscopic income to fill in the gaps which her occasional improvidence left in the housekeeping allowance."

Thanks to the generosity of their parishioners, the Carters were loaned houses in different summer resorts; Newport, Rockport, West Chop on the Vineyard, Southwest Harbor, Maine, a ranch in California, the White Mountains and at the Rangeley Lakes. Their favorite retreat, though, was their own small fishing camp at Lake Honadaga in the Adirondacks. A part of each summer was also spent with Mary at Sunnycliffe. The boys bunked together in jumbled fashion, raced around the house and romped on the beach getting into whatever mischief they could find. Norris Oliver, their older cousin whom they idolized, was often called upon to keep them in line. Sallie Carter and Katharine Oliver were just the same age, both musical and intellectual, and somewhat scornful of the "little boy's pranks." These "little boys," however, went on to distinguished careers. Two joined the Foreign Service. One was a political

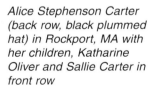

*Alice Stephenson Carter (back row, black plummed hat) in Rockport, MA with her children, Katharine Oliver and Sallie Carter in front row*

writer during the Roosevelt era, and another became a minister. After years of marriage and motherhood, Sallie threw it all aside and moved to Juneau, Alaska where she taught music and piano at local schools. In the last years of her life she changed her name to "Sister Trinity" and devoted herself to the Episcopal church.

Motherhood was hard work and eventually took its toll on Alice. Her health deteriorated and she had no strength to resist a long and painful attack of sleeping sickness from which she died in 1924. In her eulogy, delivered by Bishop Lawrence, he described a crowded, overheated confirmation service in Fall River. "The air," he said,"was intensely oppressive, but no one moved. When Mrs. Carter stepped out into the aisle, walked around the back of the pews, and threw open the windows, men, women and children lived again. That was the life work of Alice Carter. From childhood to the end, she was throwing open windows so that the light, life, cheer and heaven's radiance might shine in." John Carter was shattered when Alice died for he had adored his loving and lively wife. He lived on in Williamstown until his death in 1948.

Katharine Schermerhorn Henry, known as Katie to her family and Tante to her nieces, nephews and grandchildren, was the prettiest Henry girl with wavy blonde hair, fair skin and bright blue eyes. Her features were soft, her manner loving and gentle, and she had a quiet, firm faith in herself and in the world, not unlike her mother's. She and Alice were closest in age and for a time, John Carter was smitten with both of them and not sure which one he wanted to marry. He chose Alice while Katie married Robert Storer Stephenson, a cheerful and attractive architect from New Jersey.

Katharine Henry Stephenson with her granddaughter, Katrina Leeb Debevoise

Rob Stephenson's health was delicate and the family doctor cautioned Katharine not to marry and have children with him. She ignored this well-meant advice and they were wed on June 1, 1898. The Stephensons moved into a house in South Orange and had five children, some of whom proved the doctor's warning correct.

George, the eldest, escaped medical problems and was handsome, gregarious, and full of fun. At Princeton during the 1920's, he was the perfect personification of F. Scott Fitzgerald's "college man." Upon graduation, he joined a banking house in New York and married the red-haired daughter of Princeton's Dean Gauss. When his niece, Katrina Leeb and I were teenagers, we both had violent crushes on George. We were thrilled when he teased and flirted with us, and made up our minds to find husbands *just* like him.

Mary, called Polly, had epilepsy, a disease that in her day carried a social stigma based primarily on ignorance. Polly's "condition" wasn't talked about much and she lived most of her adult life in Vermont, in residential facilities that offered medical services. In spite of her restricted life, she had great artistic flair, a good sense of humor, and a perspective that made up for the inevitable loneliness of her situation. She was very close to her family and adored her nieces and nephews with whom she kept in close touch.

Katrina Stephenson was pretty, intelligent, and gentle like her mother, with a gay spirit and zest for life. After she was graduated from Vassar, she taught school for two years before marrying tall, handsome Henry Lorent Leeb in 1924. Henry's father, Alfred Leeb, emigrated from Sweden when he was 19 and made his way to Chicago where he found a bride, Emma Philpot. The couple moved east and Alfred, with a Swedish friend, started a wine-importing firm. Their son Henry was bright and ambitious. He attended M.I.T. and after graduation accepted a job in radio manufacturing but left to join the New York Trust Company. Eventually, his career took him into the rayon industry. But it was when he retired that he was happiest. He and Katrina moved to Alfred Leeb's dairy farm in Gladstone, New Jersey which they ran successfully for decades. Henry also became an expert cabinet maker. As I write now, my word processor sits on a lovely pine table he made for my wedding. Its top is a plank from a Portland, Maine salt wharf.

*Katrina Stephenson Leeb*

In South Orange, Katrina put her time and energy into volunteer work as President of the Junior League, church auxiliaries and the Garden Club of Somerset Hills. She wrote to me that "it all sounds pretty tame compared to what your generation achieved," but anyone who has headed a volunteer organization knows that the job is all-consuming and requires a multitude of skills and disciplines — patience, tact, sensitivity and understanding. Katrina brought all those talents to her work. Although she was considered delicate in her youth, she has weathered eye problems, deafness, fractured bones, pneumonia, and assorted accidents and is today, in her nineties, a lovely person and a great-grandmother of seven. She still lives on her beloved Walnut Hill Farm in New Jersey.

I must digress for a moment from Nantucket to recall my happy memories of the farm. My mother Katharine and Katrina

Leeb were devoted first cousins and hoped that their daughters (also named Katharine and Katrina) would be good friends, too. When I was quite young, instead of going to Sunnycliffe in June, I spent a month with the Leebs in South Orange and at the farm. Indeed, Katrina and I became and still remain dearest friends. In South Orange, we learned to play tennis and swim, played in Trina's playhouse, and just enjoyed being young girls together. In the afternoon when we were supposed to be taking a nap, we'd hear the tinkle of the Good Humor truck's bell and we'd sneak out of the house to buy a toasted almond or chocolate-covered ice cream stick.

Every morning Jean, the Scottish cook, served us poached eggs which we both detested. When no one was looking, we each took the wobbly mass outside and dumped it under the drain pipe much to the delight of Trina's black cocker spaniel who made short work of this morning treat. He wasn't as fond of the buttermilk I was supposed to drink, however, nor of Jean's authentic Scotch porridge.

In 1941, Katrina and Henry Leeb, distressed with the plight of English children caught in the bombing of World War II, decided to take in two for the duration. They arrived: Patricia Jeans, 13, and her 10-year old brother Paul. The Leebs, with one daughter, were not quite prepared for a rambunctious and often unmanageable boy. It's a tribute to their love and firm discipline that both Paul and Patricia survived separation from their parents and progressed successfully through adolescence to adulthood in this country. The families became fast friends, and still are.

*Katrina Leeb and Katharine Oliver Stanley-Brown in South Orange, NJ, 1936*

After Tricia arrived, the month of June was even more fun. Aunt Trina taught the three of us to sew and supervised our first efforts: broomstick skirts of flowered cotton. When we went out to the farm we made a small contribution to the war effort by weeding the vegetable garden. We learned to skim cream from milk in the big, stainless steel separator, thus freeing farm workers from one daily chore at least. We also swam in the pond and learned to ride horses. In the long twilight of June evenings, we joined other youngsters on the farm for spirited games of "Kick the Can" and "Sardines" or went to nearby Morristown for Chinese food and a movie. Melvin Blaufuss, whose father was the resident farmer, was always ready for an adventure and drove us all in the farm truck.

During these June visits, Trina and I usually spent a week with her grandmother, Tante, who by then lived in Westport, Connecticut. Grape vines and wisteria laced the terrace trellis of her two-story shingled house, and the air was heavy with the scent of lilac and the insistent buzz of bumblebees. Each year, waiting for us on the twin beds of the third floor guestroom under the eaves, were identical smocked dresses of checked cotton. The whole front from neck to waist was gathered, in Tante's meticulous hand, with rows of tiny stitches that puckered the material into a pattern. Cross or blanket stitches edged the white sleeve cuffs and round collar. One year the dresses were blue and white; the next, pink, lavender or green. At the waist, a set-in sash formed a large bow at the back. And the hems were generous enough to anticipate a year's growth. I loved the dresses which, I felt, gave me a special bond with my cousin. It was as good as having a sister. Then the summer came when Trina refused to wear the smocked dress that lay on her bed. She was a year older than I and, without my realizing it, had matured. Her growing body made it clear she could no longer wear that type of dress. We sat on the top of the roof eating fresh cucumbers out of Tante's garden and talking about boys. It would be a year before I could appreciate such a conversation, and by that time Patricia had arrived and there were three of us to share the mysterious subject of men.

Baby Alice Stephenson lived only a few years. When she was about four, the Stephensons summered in Mt. Sinai on Long Island. Close by was a farm where Alice often drank the warm, fresh but unpasteurized milk. Only she of all the children contracted tuberculosis, and without today's drugs, she died. After Alice's death, Helen Stephenson was Katie and Rob's baby. She was called Eddie and always possessed a charming "little girl" quality, perhaps because she had a slight lisp. She was deaf for much of her adult life. Pretty, outgoing, and gregarious, with a great sense of fun, Eddie attracted the attention of Cleve White, her brother George's Princeton roommate. Cleve and Eddie were married after her graduation from Connecticut College. She enjoyed being a wife and mother, and brought a nice sense of humor to married life that made it all seem fun. The Whites lived in Noroton, Connecticut and summered in West Falmouth, Massachusetts, where Cleve loved to sail. Eventually, they moved there permanently when he retired from a New York securities firm.

Returning to the Henry women, Anna Schermerhorn Henry, the adored baby girl of the family was born in 1875, when Mary was 14. Sadly, Anna never saw Nantucket as she died in 1886. The illness came on suddenly and although the doctors came twice a day, they were not sure what was wrong. It could be typhoid fever, they said, or it might be tuberculous meningitis. The Henrys felt helpless and sick at heart. After three weeks of high fever, intense headaches, pain and delirium, it was clear that Anna would not recover. Mary, who had taught Anna to read and write, was deeply affected by her little sister's illness. She wrote in her diary: "Our darling Anna can not live through the day, insensible since l a.m., took nourishment until 6 o'clock, breathed with difficulty until 1:15 when her spirit passed away. Kissed her goodbye at 12 . . . cried myself to sleep." The whole family was devastated by Anna's death, reflected by the sad entries in Mary's diary. On Christmas day that year she noted: "A truly sad morning, the first without Anna."

It is most likely that Anna died of typhoid fever, a common terror in 1886. It reached epidemic proportions in 1897 when 14,082 cases were reported in Philadelphia alone, before a serum, discovered by Sir Almoth Wright in England in 1895, provided protection. Prior to medical discoveries such as this, doctors could offer few remedies for illness. They made house calls, encouraged patients and families and offered what palliatives and analgesics they had. For a severe pain that gripped Mary for a week, Dr. Pierson prescribed laudanum, or perhaps cocaine, that made her sleep for almost twenty-four hours. Another time when she had a stomach ailment, she improved on the doctor's recommendation of raw oysters and oyster broth. In a religious family such as the Henrys, faith and prayer were often the only recourses, and they were likely to say that death was God's will.

If little Anna never saw Nantucket, all the other Henry girls and their families did. Until the four Stephenson children were married, Katie and Rob brought them to Sunnycliffe each summer. The guest book is full of their delightful poetry, Rob's often trilling on for five or six verses. In spite of being younger, both Katrina and Polly loved being with their cousin Katharine Oliver, my mother, whom they called Kot. Family friendships were very close among the many cousins, due in part to the efforts made by Mary, Alice and Katharine to bring everyone together, particularly during the summer. When my mother was growing up, a visit to the Carters in Rockport or the Adirondacks was a yearly, much-anticipated treat. And both Alice and Katharine came to Nantucket each year with their children, visits not for a day or two, but for weeks at a time during which the cousins came to know each other very well. Everyone somehow managed to squeeze into Sunnycliffe. Little boys thought it a great adventure to sleep on the back lawn in tents. The girls packed into the Nursery while their parents and whatever baby was with them, stayed in the guest room on the front of the house, next to Mary's room.

That room was one of the nicest at Sunnycliffe. Three windows, facing the ocean, formed a bay. Another window looked northeast. A small porch jutted out towards the water and when there were twin beds in the room it was almost impossible to open its door. An imaginative carpenter solved the problem by installing, instead of a swinging door, a ceiling-to-floor, double-hung window. It always seemed odd to unlock a catch, push up the lower window until it locked against a metal peg high up, and go out the window onto the porch. But it worked! This little porch was an ideal place to stretch out on the wicker chair with its own foot rest, listen to the surf, feel the gentle easterly breeze and lose oneself in a good book.

The room was a guest room, my mother's room when she outgrew the Nursery, and her room as a married woman. Eventually, it became my room. In the last generation to live at Sunnycliffe, it was my eldest niece's room. Sometimes a doll sat in a tiny wicker arm chair near the bay window with a pile of handmade doll clothes beside it. At another time, the closet was full of 1920's lounging pajamas, beach hats, and my father's box of watercolor paints.

In one corner of the room lay the manuscripts of my mother's articles and books. One several occasions, the bureau was covered with lotions, perfumes, lipstick, bobby pins, earrings and mascara as teenagers tried out new personalities in the mirror. Passionate letters were written on the green, blotting paper desk pad. Summer reading lists were completed in the wicker armchair. And dreams were dreamed with the gentle sound of the surf and the constant wind blowing through the windows.

# Chapter Four
# The Henry Men

Looking at the three Henry brothers together, you might think they were triplets, so closely did they resemble each other. They all had the prominent, straight Henry nose, close, deep-set blue eyes and full lips that, at rest, were just short of a smile. All three parted their dark hair in the middle and were clean-shaven as was the fashion for young men at the turn of the century. The Henry face suggested languor rather than vitality, soft thoughtfulness rather than action, but in fact, all three brothers were energetic, athletic and hard-working.

Edward Henry was born in 1863, two years after Mary. He was an earnest boy who took his position as oldest son seriously. He was thrilled to pass the entrance examinations for Yale, but when it developed that there wasn't enough money for Edward's tuition as long as his father, Lewis, was trying to pay back his business losses, Edward gallantly forfeited his place and joined the family firm as a sugar broker. Monday through Friday, steel-rimmed glasses on his nearset eyes, and dressed in a dark, three-piece suit, stiff collar and polished shoes, Edward took the train to Hoboken, the ferry to New York, and then the trolley to the office.

*Edward Schermerhorn Henry, 1863—1904*

He found fun and companionship where he could. He knew his sisters' girl friends, but he usually played tennis, billiards, attended concerts and opera with men. In the spring and fall he played baseball or football after work in Newark and Hoboken. A thoughtful friend, Dan Geer, sent him a subscription to the *Yale Daily News*, and many weekends found Edward in blazer, striped pants and straw boater, joining his friends in New Haven for football games or crew races. At home, he spent his free time with his family and at church. He sang with groups at several churches, was a faithful parishioner of Grace Church in Orange, and gathered greens and helped trim the church tree at Christmas.

But there was more to Edward's life than perhaps his family knew. At least I hope so!  In such a close-knit family it was hard to get away from his sisters' scrutiny. Mary took an inordinate interest in his comings and goings. In 1883 (Edward was then 20) she wrote in her diary "Edward did not come home tonight (Feb. 15), "Edward came home from Newark where he spent last night" (Feb. 25), "Edward did not come home" (Feb. 26), and "Edward at home for a wonder" (Feb. 27). On March 10 she noted: "Edward, as usual, not home tonight. Louise stayed awake for him." Poor young man, he couldn't escape his sharp-eyed sisters long enough to have an affair if he wanted to. As it was, he never married, and he had bad luck in business. Several times between 1883 and 1886, Mary wrote that Edward "lost his place", but he never lacked for cheerful optimism and faith.

Then suddenly at the age of 41, Edward died. One family story was that, singing hymns while running to catch a train, he had fallen into a ditch and died of heart failure. There's another story, too, only a bit less dramatic. With a shortage of rooms, Edward and his younger brother Jay, shared a bed in the house at East Orange. On the morning of October 25, 1904, Jay awoke to find his brother dead beside him. The shock of it, my mother told me, turned his black hair white in a day. The *Orange Chronicle*, however, attributed Edward's death to an attack of indigestion followed by heart failure. "Funeral services," the paper continued, "were held in Grace Church, nearly a thousand persons being present." Many of those were Edward's friends from the Hope Lodge, F and A.M. of East Orange, the Baltusrol Golf Club, the Republican Club of East Orange, New York Society, Sons of the Revolution, and the Mummers. Others were fellow singers from St. Mark's Church in West Orange, Dr. John Hall's church in New York and the Mendelssohn Union of Orange. The *Chronicle* noted that Edward was "well known in the Oranges, his friends were legion and his death will create a void in many a circle." Musical, gregarious, athletic and cheerful, he combined the best Henry attributes. After him, a sister or niece might be musical, another athletic, another devoted to charitable or church works, but in no other family member would so many charming qualities be united.

Lewis Chauncey Henry, the only one of the eight Henry children whose middle name wasn't Schermerhorn, was born on November 6, 1872. He was an imp, mischievous, full of fun and pranks, the joker of the family. Broad humor was his trademark. Very much like Edward in looks, he too was outgoing and athletic, and admired by friends and family all his life. Although he lacked Edward's true musical talent, he often broke into emotional renditions of opera arias or songs by Sigmund Romberg, ignoring the groans of his family. Like Edward, Lewie was accepted at Yale, but again put duty first

and joined his father's sugar business. He was a natural sales-
man whose personal charm and innate business sense helped
bring Lewis B. Henry & Sons into the 20th century. His nephew
John Carter recalled that "Uncle Lewis would take my sister
Sallie and me to wholesale candy stores in New York City, and
order boxes pulled out and given to us for our delectation. He
used to take us driving up Broadway in a hansom cab and
wave and bow greetings to all the girls. This used to impress us
for they invariably smiled and waved back to him and we
thought it was wonderful that he knew so many ladies."

*Lewis Chauncey Henry
with Katharine Oliver in
1908*

Lewie had a strong sense of family responsibility, particularly for his sister Mary. He not only supported her financially
after her divorce, but surprised her with lavish presents, trips to
Europe, opera and concert tickets and dinners in New York.
Best of all for Mary, he made Nantucket summers at Sunnycliffe
possible. It was Lewie who put electricity in the house, added a
guest room, provided Mary with her own bathroom, paid for
maids and nurses and, generally, made her life easier. He loved
being ahead of the pack — the first one to own a new stove,
refrigerator or washing machine. He was one of the first summer residents to bring a car to Nantucket, and an early com-
muter by plane.

My mother was Lewie's special favorite. She remembered
both her uncles Edward and Lewie when she and her mother
and brother moved back to live in East Orange. They were
exciting companions who "thought nothing of bicycling up
Orange mountain back of Llewellyn Park and back, refreshing
themselves with a beer or two at the top." She recalled Lewie's
lavish parties in New York at the old, cavernous brownstone
Belmont Hotel and the new Waldorf, or at The Banker's Club

*Mary's new room and
porch at Sunnycliffe*

on Wall Street. And, there was one special memory from her youth.

One day in 1909 when she was 17, Lewie invited her and five of her friends to spend the day with him at Coney Island. The girls and Lewie took the train from Orange to Hoboken, the ferry to New York and then the subway to Coney Island. There was a roller coaster, a small zoo, a Merry-Go-Round and lots of shooting galleries. The girls tried everything, reveled in a huge lunch at the hotel on the beach, and set off for a walk. Coming out of the hotel, my mother wrote, "I was surprised to see a zebra wandering down the middle of the road near us. Uncle Lewie had an Eastman Kodak box camera and, calling to him to take our picture, I walked quietly up to the zebra and hung my arm around his neck. He gazed at me benignly and seemed to enjoy the whole affair when suddenly his purple-faced and puffing owner came running into view and said: "I've been chasing that damned zebra all morning every since he got out of his cage, and now you have caught him! How many are there of you? Seven? Well, I'll get you all free passes for the whole place!"

During the 1920's and 1930's, Lewie made and lost several small fortunes playing the stock market. While his family disapproved of this behavior, they were secretly thrilled with his glamorous and unorthodox money-making. In the business world, he was completely scrupulous and did very well. When Lewie had money he threw it around generously. "Here," he'd say to my mother, tossing a 10 dollar bill onto her bureau in Sconset, "buy yourself a new hat." In June, 1930, Lewie arrived on the Island with a crate of melons, a crate of peaches and a crate of oranges for Mary. Another day in Town, he bought a sheaf of day lilies from the Bartlett farm truck and gave one to each lady he met on the Main Street. After Mary developed diabetes in 1931, Lewie surprised her with a week at the Dennis Hotel in Atlantic City. When his brother Jay needed an operation that same year, Lewie paid for his private room at the then exorbitant rate of $20 a day. He loved the impetuous gesture, and equally, the grateful thanks.

But everything didn't always work out as nicely. In 1932, when my mother and father considered moving to Nantucket permanently, Lewie offered to buy them a house. Business was going well. They were thrilled and found a perfect gem on New Dollar Lane in Town. Negotiations began but at the last moment Lewie took back the offer. Business reversals, he said. My parents were shattered but Lewie, as he did in lean times, tightened his belt, called up his gaiety and optimistic spirit and hoped things would come right again in time.

There was also a price to pay, albeit small, for Lewie's kindness. Often, after astounding the family with his largess, he would ask for weeks afterwards: "Did you like my present?" Or, "What did you think of the dishwasher I gave you? You haven't mentioned it." He seemed to need constant reinforcement that his family depended on him and that they loved him. He should have known that money didn't buy affection. Everyone loved him for himself.

Like all the Henrys, Lewie was emotional and romantic, but never truly in love until he was 38 years old when he met beautiful, auburn-haired Margaret Scranton, the eldest daughter of a wealthy and successful retired coal operator from Scranton, Pennsylvania. When Lewie finally proposed to Margaret and was accepted, the shock of the surprise was so great that he was immediately ill. His brand-new fiancee and her parents spent the whole night ministering to the "Henry Stomach" which could be counted upon to react violently to any emotion.

*Margaret Scranton*

Margaret was tall, handsome, athletic and a superb horse-woman. She and Lewie made a dashing pair. After their marriage in 1910, according to John Carter's amusing story of the family, *The Rectory*, Lewie was said to have discovered that Margaret's beautiful hair was not her own but a wig, hers having been lost during a typhoid attack. A further blow, as John Carter explained in his book, was that old Mr. Scranton lost all his money in a business deal so that Margaret's inheritance evaporated. But neither revelation dampened Lewie's love or enthusiasm.

The young Henrys moved into their own house in South Orange and made yearly visits to Sunnycliffe where, with his usual generosity, Lewie financed the construction of a large, double bedroom for their use. Jutting out to the north, with views of the Bluff, the ocean and sunrise to the east, and the moors and sunset to the west, the room was one of the nicest in the house. Lewie and Margaret usually came to Sconset in September or October when the Island was at its most brilliant and largely deserted. It was the time they liked best, as they noted in the guest book. In 1916, Lewie wrote "Every year my love grows stronger for Sconset" and Margaret added "Three perfect weeks at Sunnycliffe." In September, 1917, Lewie was moved to write "If Heaven is not to be my lot, may faithful Sconset be the spot." And in 1918, "Two weeks in an earthly Heaven" from Lewie and "Days of perfect happiness" from

*Lewis C. Henry at his Shimmo house — 1956*

Margaret. In the mid-1920's, Lewie bought land in Shimmo, a small community facing Nantucket harbor, where he built Enchantment, on the edge of the bluff. At vast cost and much complaint on his part, he added a bulkhead to protect the bluff and the house from erosion. Without it, Enchantment might have slid into the harbor. Known as an "upside-down house", the bedrooms, dining room and kitchen were on the ground floor. The second floor living room across the whole front of the house provided an unobstructed view of Nantucket town, incoming steamboats, fishing boats and sailboat races.

Margaret's younger sister Madeleine Scranton was married in 1913 to Beverly Chew, an old and dear friend of Lewie's from South Orange. Madeleine, like Margaret, was strikingly beautiful and the two sisters were very alike. Without children, and living close to each other, the Lewis Henrys and the Beverly Chews were an intimate foursome who shared vacations together in Sconset and happy times in South Orange. In the early 1920's, the Chews moved to Geneva, New York and in 1927, most unexpectedly, Madeleine Chew died.

That summer Lewie came twice to Sunnycliffe alone, fueling gossip behind the bathroom door that things weren't right between the young Henrys. In the fall of 1928, Margaret startled the family by announcing that, after 18 years of marriage, she was pregnant. By summer of 1929, Margaret was living in Geneva, New York where in July, her daughter Madeleine Woodbridge was born. My mother wrote to my father: "Lewie's daughter is fine . . . very strong and beautifully formed. Margaret has had the stitches out and is doing splendidly." Another letter the end of July reads: "Lewie is being sweet — loads of fun, perfectly happy-acting and not a word of Margaret or baby. Has not been to Geneva all summer! I think he has made up his mind to come to Nantucket and stay, and to be just as independent as she is."

Independent or not, Lewie, Margaret and baby Madeleine were living in South Orange on June 5, 1930 when Katharine wrote from East Orange: "Drove out to see Margaret and baby. She is handsome, very red hair and healthy. Margaret spent her time telling me how deceitful Mrs. P. (nurse) is."

At a family wedding the next June Lewie, perhaps pining for Margaret who had gone to Geneva with the baby that morning, reportedly drank too much and passed out. Then in March of 1931, my mother wrote to my father from East Orange: "Lewie is really going to divorce Margaret, you will be glad to know! And she says she is to marry Bev who will adopt the child." A week later Margaret came to New York to stay at the Algonquin Hotel while she settled details of the divorce. Lewie appeared to be in fine spirits, my mother reports, wanted to give her a cash settlement, sell the South Orange house and give her the furniture and put his own things in his Nantucket house.

Lewie never said a word against Margaret or Beverly. The whole marriage with all its heartaches was swept away and Lewie returned, at least outwardly to his usual ebullient, optimistic self. Curiously, in his 1959 obituary, the Nantucket *Inquirer and Mirror* stated that "a daughter, Madeleine W. Henry of Geneva, N.Y. is listed as an heir-at-law in the petition for allowance, but no bequests were left her under terms of the will."

Margaret Scranton Henry Chew died in 1941 in Geneva, New York where she and Beverly had lived for many years. Beverly Chew died in 1972, ending a mysterious tangle of lives, dates and events.

Jacob Schermerhorn was the youngest Henry boy. Born in South Orange in 1876, he and his sister Anna were the babies, petted and pampered by older sisters and brothers during their childhoods. Happily, the Henry finances improved and Jay was able to go to college. He chose Stevens Institute in Newark and graduated as a civil engineer. Right out of college he joined a firm that sold lighting equipment to railroad companies and stayed with them until he retired. Jay didn't have Edward's musical talent, nor was he as outgoing, amusing and charming as Lewie. Endowed with average intelligence, and always

*The golfers, Jacob Schermerhorn Henry and Lewis Chauncey Henry*

somewhat in Lewie's shadow, Jay was nonetheless, a popular member of the "younger set." He was an avid athlete and an early photograph shows him in knickers, knee socks and tweed jacket, poised at the edge of Sunnycliffe's bluff, with his golf club on the upswing. After Lewie's divorce, he and Jay were inseparable. They both lived and commuted from the East Orange house to New York, shared Enchantment, and enjoyed many of the same friends.

*Jay with his new "motor-car," circa 1907*

Jay spent a lifetime trying to be like his older brother. When I was young, I remember them both stopping at Sunnycliffe on their way to a golf game. They looked like Tweedledum and Tweedledee — both portly gentlemen with white hair parted in the middle and wearing round steel-rimmed glasses. They sported natty pastel linen trousers, open polo shirts and spiked golf shoes. Lewie was somehow snappier, cracked jokes, and constantly jingled coins in his pants pocket. Jay had a quieter Puckish humor. When my mother and I visited in East Orange, Jay and Lewie were still working in New York. In the late afternoon they appeared, looking like twins in their double-breasted, dark suits and white shirts with stiff, starched collars. After greeting the family, they both disappeared into the study at the back of the house with its dark furniture and rose damask wallpaper. Jay would unlock the glass doors of the secretary to lift out a bottle of Wild Turkey bourbon. Brown, the butler, magically appeared with a tray of glasses and bucket of ice. Holding a tumbler up to the light, Jay poured a generous but careful two ounces, added four ice cubes and handed the glass to Lewie who contributed a splash of water. Each of them, with glass and evening newspaper in hand, went to his favorite stuffed chair to unwind from the rigors of New York. Lewie, in particular, was an avid newspaper reader. When I came to say goodnight to him in his bedroom where he went right after dinner, I would find him, sprawled out on top of the bed in bright, satin pajamas with two or three newspapers spread out around him. He never read for pleasure, unless following the stock market or the race track could be called pleasure. He loved people and he loved action. He was a doer rather than a thinker.

In one area, Jay simply couldn't compete with Lewie — wooing women. Lewie toyed with women as he toyed with the stock market. Not so with Jay. He had only one love in his life, a married woman named Jessie for whom he pined and waited nearly 20 years. Finally, at a proper interval after Jessie's husband died, she and Jay were married. They were both in their sixties and she was the best thing that happened to him. For the years they had together he became romantic, rejuvenated and happier than he had ever been. They took a town house in

South Orange, played bridge, Canasta and golf, and spent vacations at Enchantment. After Jessie died, Jay moved back to the East Orange house and, once more, became Lewie's companion.

Before his happy marriage, Jay weathered some personal storms. At one point during the late 1940's, after his doctor told him that he was too fat and his blood pressure was alarmingly high, Jay enrolled in the new Rice Diet program at Duke University in Durham, North Carolina. For months afterwards, he lived on grapefruit and rice, though it was not obvious to the family that he lost much weight. When I was still in college in the late 1940's, my mother wrote that Jay had been taken to the Institute for Living in Hartford, Connecticut, under rather mysterious circumstances. Only much later did I learn that it was because Jay had tried to kill himself. The bullets, green with age and their powder useless, never penetrated his skull. But, since attempted suicide is illegal, the deed was reported to the police and Jay was required to undergo psychiatric evaluation and rehabilitation.

In 1946, Jay suffered a stroke and was taken to the Nantucket Cottage Hospital. After the pessimistic doctor predicted that Jay wouldn't last the night, Lewie made the necessary arrangements with Mr. Lewis, the funeral director. Mr. Lewis, in turn, called the appropriate funeral service in East Orange to alert them to the burial. By morning Jay was almost completely recovered and Lewie had to call Mr. Lewis to say "We need to postpone the arrangements." Jay lived in good health for 12 more years.

On Nantucket, both Jay and Lewie drove their large black Packards all over the Island. Jay was timid and drove very slowly, but Lewie, who still had a license at 85, drove with abandon although he could barely see or hear. When a car tried to pass him on the two-lane Long Road to Town he would roll down the window, lean on the horn and shout "You prune!" Or, if someone drove too slowly, he'd yell "Get a horse", as he passed, often on a solid double-lined stretch of winding road. It was only after he had hit a stone pillar a number of times at the summer barracks of the Massachusetts State Police and knocked down its sign, that Lewie's license was revoked. From then on he hired a young Nantucketer to drive him around the Island he loved.

When they died, Jay at 82 and Lewie a year later at 87, the family lost two more of its most colorful members.

*Lewie (76 yrs.) and Katharine (80 yrs.) in 1948*

# Chapter Five
## George's Creation

While Charles and Mary prepared for the birth of their first child, George Gibbs was busy at Nantucket. In June, 1889, the Olivers with two-month old Norris made their first trip to the Island. Mr. Gibbs met the steamer and drove them in his carriage to their new house in Siasconset. Among the handful of others, it stood out as its new white cedar shingles had yet no time to weather. Not everyone wanted a cottage on the windswept North Bluff. The houses were built of wood and heated with open fires, and the nearest fire wagon was nine miles away. It was safer to live in Town.

"Good heavens!" exclaimed Charles when he saw the house. "I had no idea it would be so large."

"Well, Dr. Oliver," said Mr. Gibbs, "I knew you summer folks wouldn't be happy with a little cottage like the ones in the village. You'd want a fine house like the ones in Narragansett Pier or Newport, and that's what you have! Besides, there was all that money in the bank. I had to use it up!"

The house was splendid, indeed. It was large and square, three stories high, facing eastward towards the ocean, but far enough back from the bluff to leave a spacious front lawn. There were three brick chimneys, porches all around the ground floor, and the shutters and trim, like those of other 'Sconset houses, were dark green. Behind the house, on the street side, stood a wood house, a tool shed, and an outhouse.

Inside, all the walls were paneled as were the ceilings with tongue and groove white pine. Each of the fire places was equipped with interesting andirons and fire tools. In the living room, cast-iron owls with amber eyes that glowed in the fire held the logs, and in the dining room red-coated Hessian soldiers provided the same service.

The living room ran across the entire front of the house and from it there were magnificent views of the ocean. Off it, a short hall led to the dining room on the left, and to a medical office for Charles on the right. Off the office was a warm and always sunny glassed-in porch with windows facing east, north and west. Beyond the hall was the large kitchen dominated by a familiar brand of coal stove, a Florence. Then came a pantry, and a laundry room. Mr. Gibbs had purchased elaborate stained wicker furniture and Oriental scatter rugs for the living room, and substantial dark blue furniture for the dining room.

On the second floor were two double bedrooms, a tiny single room and a nursery, all with lovely views of the sea or the moors to the west. Like the downstairs, the upstairs rooms were also pine-paneled. Each contained white iron beds covered with fresh white cotton spreads, painted wooden bureaus and desks and white wicker armchairs. On the floors there were hooked rugs. Thin, ruffled curtains fluttered at the windows, light enough to let in sunshine without spoiling the view. An atmosphere of summer pervaded the house.

Under the eaves on the third floor were two tiny rooms for servants and for storage. Mr. Gibbs had thought of everything. All the Olivers had to do was to move in.

"I notice," Mary said to Charles, "that each house in Sconset has a name. What shall ours be?" As they looked around, it came immediately to mind. The first rays of sunlight each morning touched the bluff that fell away to the beach — the house would be called Sunnycliffe.

Long before Sunnycliffe was built, Siasconset was a summer outpost for Nantucket fishermen. In the seventeenth century, men left Nantucket Town to fish for cod and bluefish across the Island, and as they spent long hours away from home, they built themselves "fishing stands" out of whatever pieces of driftwood they found washed up on the beach. These were crude shacks of one room with board chimneys, fire traps at best. The men cooked on an open porch and didn't care much how they lived. It was their escape from females and domesticity. In time, of course, their wives were curious. What was so enticing about Sconset? So they joined their menfolk and, like women throughout history, went about improving living conditions. They insisted on proper chimneys, indoor kitchens, and bedrooms. The additions were called "warts" and were often only wide enough for a single bed. A straight ladder, fastened to the wall, led to an attic where the children slept, often two or three abreast. This area below the village bluff, near the beach, soon became known as Codfish Park. Gradually, more houses were constructed above the bank on Main Street. They were low, shingled, and surrounded by white fences enclosing tiny gardens of bright nasturtiums, marigold, Dusty Miller and daisies. In June, wild roses rambled over the walls and roofs. Many of the cottages had blue shutters which, according to tradition dating from the eighteenth century, showed that the houses belonged to ship captains and first officers.

By contrast, the houses in Town were grander and reflected the fortunes of successful whaling families. In 1770, Nantucket's fleet of 125 vessels was supreme in the industry, bringing in that year 14,331 barrels of sperm oil. From then until almost 1860, Nantucket enjoyed a period of splendor as the foremost whaling port of New England. During the 1830's and 1840's, the handsome mansions of brick and clapboard, with their Greek-revival doorways, built on Nantucket's Main Street were symbols of the Island's prosperity. Many of these majestic houses still stand today.

Unfortunately, it was the appearance of larger whaling ships that signaled the decline of Nantucket's chief industry. A sand bar stretching from Madaket on the western end of the Island to Great Point along Nantucket's north shore, shoaled to a depth of six feet at low water at the mouth of the inner harbor. Small whalers could cross it without a problem, but larger ships were unable to enter and had to anchor outside in an open roadstead. Offloading sperm oil was difficult if not impossible in bad weather, and gradually ships took their cargo to the more convenient port of New Bedford. By 1857, there were 95 whaling ships hailing from New Bedford and just four from Nantucket.

Between 1840 and 1860, four events occured which changed the face of Nantucket forever. First, in 1846, the worst fire in the Island's history broke out in the business district. It soon spread to shops, houses, and stored oil barrels, ultimately destroying 360 buildings over a 36-acre area. Damage totaled more than a million dollars and, as insurance covered only two-thirds of the loss, some merchants never recovered.

Second, in 1849, gold was discovered in California. It was Westward Ho! for young and eager Nantucketers who deserted the then dying whaling industry for the prospect of instant wealth. Scores of them never returned.

The third blow, which would affect more than Nantucket's economy, was the discovery of coal oil in Pennsylvania in the 1860's which led to the manufacture of kerosene. It was cheaper to obtain and produce than sperm oil, and better for lighting as well and its popularity doomed what was left of the whaling industry.

The Civil War also took its toll on island commerce as Confederate raiders captured and destroyed Yankee vessels up and down the coast.

By the 1870's, however, a new era was beginning as the concept of owning a summer home intrigued thousands of urban Americans. As cities grew and industrialization flourished, so did pollution, noise and filth. Health was a major concern for middle and upper income families who wanted to take their children away from smoke and disease. With money to spend on themselves, they were drawn to the country — the mountains, the lakes, the coast and islands away from the fetid atmosphere of the cities. With its pure air, warm, clean water and delightful tranquility, Nantucket seemed like paradise.

The wave of new summer residents came from the Midwest and the East by train and by boat with trunks of linen, blankets and clothing as well as books and servants. Like the Olivers they built houses, hired cooks, handy men and drivers for their three-month stays. They brought city ideas to the Island but found instead to their happy surprise that the joy of Nantucket was its peacefulness and simplicity. They learned to appreciate the pleasures of nature and the Island's gentle, unhurried pace of life. They heard the gulls and terns as they wheeled overhead. They were lulled to sleep by the constant but gentle wind. They planted trumpet vine and clematis on the trellises of their summer cottages, bathed in water warmed by the Gulf Stream and walked on the lonely moors. By 1889, Sconset could boast of many new houses, but Sunnycliffe was surely one of the grander "summer cottages" on the North Bluff.

# Chapter Six
# The Parlor

Nowadays we call it the living room, but in 1889 it was "The Parlor." A large double room running across the front of the house, with a splendid view of the Bluff and the Atlantic ocean beyond, it was the focal point of activity for the Olivers. Walls, ceilings and floor were of white pine stained medium golden brown which did make the room rather dark and gloomy. Visitors entered the parlor from the front porch through a double-hung Dutch front door whose upper half was a pane of clear glass framed with colored glass squares. Straight ahead was Charles' dark, upright piano and caned, bentwood, straight-back chair. He was a serious musician who every Sunday night in Philadelphia, played Beethoven, Schubert, Schumann and Mozart with his colleagues, Dr. George Piersol, head of Gross Anatomy at the University, Dr. deSchwienitz and Dr. Kean. On vacation, Charles played the piano regularly for pleasure or accompanied Mary when she sang.

In the middle of the room stood a solid wooden table piled with books, medical journals, a kerosene lamp with a white

*Parlor at Sunnycliffe with Charles' piano*

china dome, and vases filled with wildflowers that Mary enjoyed picking. A wicker loveseat and three small chairs stood near by.

If one end of the room reflected Charles' tastes, the other belonged to Mary. She was particularly fond of the Turkish Corner whose main feature was a day-bed covered with dark red, richly patterned material. Huge pillows in vivid patterns were scattered at its head and a mohair throw rested at its foot. Oriental draperies adorned the walls behind the bed. Mary, often in a long white lawn dress, white stockings and shoes, rested there, a book of poetry in her hand. Across from the Turkish Corner was a wicker sofa, a bookcase, and a bearskin rug, head and all, whose origin has always been a mystery. The sofa faced the red brick fireplace, its frame a wooden mantel supported by two carved wooden pillars twisted to resemble ship's rope. A nice touch from George Gibbs, former ship's carpenter. Hanging on one side of the fireplace was a set of bellows, and beyond the fire tools was a fat, rush basket full of logs and kindling, much of which was driftwood from the beach. In front of the fireplace, out of reach of cinders and sparks, a sizable Oriental rug softened the bare floor.

The parlor and the dining room, which were most frequently used and seen by visitors, were the most lavishly furnished rooms at Sunnycliffe. The rest of the house was spartan with bedrooms containing only what was necessary. But that was as it should be as Mary loved entertaining, especially members of her large family who came for long visits each year. Her impromptu parties would be a nightmare for the staff eventual-

*Parlor at Sunnycliffe with Turkish corner, 1888*

37

ly, but house guests were more predictable and easier to accommodate.

In 1895, Mary acquired a guest book and encouraged each departing visitor to note his or her stay with a line or two. Parts of hymns, stanzas of poetry, and original light verse filled the early pages of the book, as did exaggerated phrases of Victorian sentiment. There were even a few sketches. If creativity failed, the least a guest could do was sign his or her name and mark the date. The comments all share the feeling that Sconset and Sunnycliffe offered a special, elusive ambience that would remain in their minds and hearts forever. The words also expressed love and admiration for Mary, a charming and attentive hostess. First to register in 1895, was Mary's widowed mother, Catherine E. Henry, who wrote:

> Sweet is the smile of home, the mutual look
>     When hearts are of each other sure:
> Sweet are the joys that crowd the household nook
>     The haunt of all affections pure.

Indeed, at the end of the nineteenth century, life for the Olivers was sweet and happy. Mary and Charles had two children, Norris aged seven, and Katharine, my mother, aged three. A nurse was present to help with their care. Sylvanus Johnson, the Olivers' black butler from Philadelphia lived on the third floor and helped run the household. The Scotch broom that Mary had planted at the edge of the Bluff was bursting with yellow blossoms. Her trellised clematis and trumpet vine were luxuriant. Mary's younger brothers, Edward, Jacob and Lewis, all came to visit, as did her sisters Katharine and Alice. The eldest Henry, however, Louisa, lived with her grandmother Louisa Barber Schermerhorn in upstate New York, and so seldom came to the Island.

During the day everyone sat on the porch talking, went to the beach, drove in the carriage to visit friends, or walked, often to the lighthouse at Sankaty. In the evening they gathered in the parlor to play Parcheesi and to enjoy the stereopticon, a hand-held instrument that displayed photographs in three dimension. A track projecting in front of the two eye pieces held a rack. A card containing duplicate, identically-sized photos was slipped into the rack which the viewer then moved forward or back until the two images merged, creating a single picture. Its depth gave it a reality that was fascinating. The Olivers had a boxful of stereoscope photographs: the Sphinx and Pyramids, camels at an oasis, the great mosque in Constantinople, the Leaning

Tower of Pisa, the Matterhorn and grape-pickers in Tuscany, all in sepia tones. Peering into the stereopticon was almost as exciting as touring the world and seeing the sights in person. And without the wonders of movies or television, the magical scenes gave the would-be travelers vicarious delight.

Mary was not only musical, she was an imaginative writer. When her children were young she created short stories for them, full of whimsical fairy-tale characters. She usually managed to slip in a moral lesson that subtly found its mark as she read the stories aloud.

In the 1920's Mah Jongg was the latest rage in the game world. One of Mary's good friends, Dr. Willy Roberts, served as a missionary to China and, on a trip back home, brought her a beautiful set that took its proud place on the living room table. Inside the handsome, black, carved box were ivory and ebony tiles. The writing and numbers in Chinese characters were etched into the ivory in red, green and black. Happily, a set of instructions, written in English, was included.

During my childhood, chess and Pick-Up Sticks joined all the other games in a large closet in the telephone room, once Dr. Oliver's office. In the late 1930's and early 1940's, the favorite was Monopoly. It was usually during a three-day northeaster that my friends and I would set the board up on the living room floor (no longer the parlor) and engage in a cutthroat battle of buying and selling. Fortunes came and went as we haggled over railroads, red, yellow, green or blue streets and gratefully accepted $200 each time we passed GO.

By 1950, my mother and her friends had become deadly serious about Scrabble. Equipped with a special dictionary, they played once or twice a week and kept a running tally all summer. I suspect that my mother usually won because as a writer, she had a large and esoteric vocabulary!

When the fog rolled in and the house was damp and clammy, the living room fire was lit. As the fire died down and the coals glowed, someone in every generation was sure to suggest toasting marshmallows. Next to the rush basket of firewood stood two long metal forks with tiny, sharp tines. Mary and her siblings kneeled in front of the fire, as I did two generations later, holding forks close to the coals until our foreheads and cheeks burned from the heat as we watched the white squares soften, lose their shape and turn brown all over. The trick was to take your marshmallow out before it dropped into the fire, bite off the crisp coating and let the still-firm inside melt in your mouth.

Some nights the wind blew from the northeast and the barometer on the wall told us that bad weather was on the way, with its wind and pelting rain. The living room always leaked, and when it did kitchen pots were placed under the white spots on the ceiling which marked where water had entered earlier. In the morning there were often dark wet spots on the carpet from new leaks undiscoverd the night before.

One particular evening in the early 1940's, the storm in the offing wasn't a northeaster, but a hurricane. My mother and I were alone at Sunnycliffe and spent the day bringing in the porch furniture, cooking food and finding flashlights and candles in case we lost electricity. Just as the wind started to rise the telephone rang. It was my mother's best friend Dolly Caracciolo who lived in Town.

"Cot, dear," she said, "I'm paralyzed with fear over here alone. May I drive over and stay with you?"

"Of course, Dolly," said my mother, "but make sure your house is locked. Oh, and don't forget to crack the windows so the wind can blow through."

"Thank you, dear" said a relieved Dolly, "Stephano and I'll be right over."

Stephano was the name of Dolly's cat named for some odd reason for her ex-husband, an Italian prince. My mother hated cats, but could hardly refuse to shelter poor Stephano in a hurricane.

*Best friends, Dorothy Adriance and Katharine Oliver in 1900*

Over Dolly came in her blue Ford coupe, clutching
Stephano and a small suitcase full of old and beautiful jewels,
given to her by the prince and his relatives when he and Dolly
were married. At the height of the storm that night, with the
house creaking, the wind howling and every pot collecting
water from the leaks, I remember Dolly lying on the living
room sofa with all her Italian jewelry clasped to her chest.

"If I'm going to die," she moaned, "I will have my best jewelry on!"

Over the years, the living room at Sunnycliffe stayed much
the same. The wicker furniture still looks elegant even now in
my brother's house and mine. Green patterned carpets did
replace the Oriental rugs. Stuffed chairs and sofas provided less
austere seating. And electricity made evenings more cheerful.
What had been a simple summer cottage came to look like a
comfortable, country home. But the feeling of Sunnycliffe was
still there. The books I read were the same my grandmother had
enjoyed, and the fresh bay leaves in a green china pot continued
to bring the fragrance of the Nantucket moors into the house.

# Chapter Seven
# Life Changes

*Mary Henry Oliver*

*The Old 'Sconset Golf Club at the turn of the century*

Mary Henry Oliver was mistress of Sunnycliffe for 49 years, a job that required skill, patience and organizational acumen. In Philadelphia life was predictable. She could count on seeing the same faces each day in the kitchen, in the bedrooms and at table. During the summer, life was simply less formal. Mary sang in the choirs of both the Union Chapel at Sconset, and at Holy Trinity Church on Rittenhouse Square, but there was a world of difference between the two institutions. She visited with friends on the Island, but left her calling cards in Philadelphia. In both locations, she had a household of servants to care for her, but in Sconset she hired seasonal help who had to be trained each year.

In spite of her impetuous nature and quick temper, Mary was a kind and patient employer. Every morning the cook would come to her second floor bedroom to discuss plans for the day. Together they would agree on menus, plan the maids' work and organize the house for guests or parties. House guests always praised Mary as a wonderful hostess who provided everything for their comfort. If the weather was fine, she was ready to play golf, sail, take a brisk walk or set up for croquet. When rain threatened, she had imaginative solutions: games, carriage rides to the Whaling Museum in Town, a trip to see the waves on the South Shore or a visit to the Hidden Forest. For to Mary, life was to be enjoyed in one's smartest clothes and with one's dearest friends and family.

It is easy to see how Mary, like many American women, was influenced by the times in which she lived. During the end of the 19th century, eyes were focused on Edward, Prince of Wales, son of Queen Victoria and heir to the throne of England. Unlike his reclusive mother, the Prince set the pattern for British social behavior and precipitated the attraction that Americans had for anything British, and preferably royal. American mothers took their debutante daughters to London for the express purpose of finding them an aristocratic husband. Rich American heiresses travelled to England and married penniless lords — anything for a title. And, those like Mary Henry who stayed in the United States, took a special interest in dressing and living in the style of British royals if not quite the manner. They copied their frothy tulle hats and flowing ankle-length gowns; they had butlers and parlor maids and elaborate five-course meals that began with fresh oysters and ended with tri-fle. Their husbands wore knickers, tweed jackets and hunting caps, as did Prince Edward, and often, as he did, kept mistress-es. But Charles Oliver wasn't the Prince. He was a brilliant, ambitious and dedicated doctor whose involvement in his career left little time for companionship and family. An only child, without experience in family life and domesticity, he did not understand his young wife's needs, nor did he know how to meet them.

Mary wanted a storybook marriage — the perfect meeting of mind, body and soul. In her pale green sitting room on Locust Street, she wondered where the happy days of her engagement had gone when Charles came to Orange on week-ends and they walked together in Llewellyn Park. When Charles was invited to Vienna to lecture, Mary stayed in Philadelphia. Her children were with her, but in the care of a governess or their teachers, and so removed from her direct care. She could scarcely go out alone in the evening and, after a while, she was, frankly, bored. She missed her cozy family, her jolly, teasing brothers and her loving sisters. She thought wist-fully of special friends who used to visit and the trolley car rides she had taken to see them. And even when Charles was at home, she was jealous of the long hours of research and study which she interpreted as neglect of her and her marriage.

At first, Mary made shorts visits back to New Jersey. She wanted the children to see their grandparents. Gradually, the visits lengthened as the dissatisfaction and misunderstanding grew. One significant incident may have been the final straw. In the course of research on eye surgery, Charles had theorized that cocaine could be an effective anesthesia. Used as such, it would not enter the system as a narcotic, nor would it be addic-tive. Rather than test his new idea on patients, he dropped cocaine into his own eyes. Horrified, Mary wrote her mother: "Charlie is taking drugs."

Finally, in 1904, Mary took Norris and Katharine back to New Jersey to live. It was a bold move, one born of desperate unhappiness, misunderstanding and disillusion. Divorce was unheard of in Mary's family and not condoned easily in society at the beginning of the twentieth century. Separation wasn't much better. Mary's decision was a momentous one, and from then on life wasn't easy. She was no longer mistress of her own house; rather, a lone mother with two teenage children (Norris was 16, Katharine was 12), dependent upon the charity of her family. For weeks she lay on the chaise-longue in her third floor bedroom weeping, to the puzzled dismay of her children. How could she face the world as such a social failure? Why was she so unhappy when she had made the decision that freed her from what she thought was an untenable situation? What would she do for the rest of her life? Unwilling to see both sides of the question, Mary felt wronged and slighted. And, since little good was said of Charles, Katharine thought that her father was a "fiend incarnate" but didn't know why. Norris, who worshiped his father, became increasingly withdrawn and morose.

In 1907, Charles and Mary were legally divorced although it was not common knowledge in the family. Mary never mentioned it during her lifetime and called herself Mrs. Mary S. Oliver until her death in 1938. And, although she had many admirers, she never remarried. For Charles, life moved differently. Initially devastated by Mary's rebuff, he moved to California after the divorce to escape the painful memories of Philadelphia. In the winter of 1911, he married Miss Carrie Phoebus, a dressmaker in Los Angeles with whom he found brief happiness until his death on April 8 the same year from nephritis and pulmonary edema.

Mary's brother Lewie and her son Norris attended the memorial service at Holy Trinity in Philadelphia, which overflowed with Charles's distinguished medical colleagues. Dr. Thorington, Mary's dear friend, described the funeral to her in detail by letter. Since he knew one of the executors of Charles's will, he wrote: "I will be glad to see that you have any object which you would like to possess." In time, Mary must have made her wishes clear to Dr. Thorington, for Oliver family portraits, Dresden china, silver, books and jewelry have been passed down through her now for three generations.

When Mary's mother, Catherine Henry, died in 1913, Mary took charge of the East Orange house. Her brothers, in turn, cared for her financially and saw to it that she enjoyed a comfortable life. Lewie, by then a successful businessman, gave her a trip to Europe every two years. Mary loved the glamor of ocean liners which always included meeting new and interesting people and sitting at the Captain's Table. She always spent a few weeks in England to visit her friends the Connetts and to purchase tailor-made, tweed suits. She then took the steamer and boat train to Paris where she immersed herself in art, music

*Nantucket steamer, inbound*

and beauty. Sometimes her trips included a few weeks in Italy, but she was indifferent to Spain and Charles' ancestral home, La Coruña. It was her son Norris' lifelong wish to visit the city, a wish sadly unfulfilled. But however much Mary enjoyed foreign travel, her heart was in Nantucket and her yearly trip to the island was a grand one.

Early each June, with an assortment of relatives, at least two dozen pieces of luggage, a dog and a bird in a cage, Mary boarded the Fall River Line steamer at Pier 14 in New York. There she was ushered into a suite with living room, two bedrooms and private bath. She insisted on having dinner and breakfast served in her stateroom, not in the dining saloon. One time, dissatisfied with the location of the table in her stateroom, she demanded that the purser move it.

"But, Mrs. Oliver, the table is bolted to the floor," he replied.

"No matter, I would like it moved," was her crisp response. Although a workman was called in, the bolt wouldn't budge and the table stayed where it was much to Mary's annoyance.

Mary was a good sailor and didn't mind how rough the seas got as they often did on Long Island Sound. When I was eight, I was with her on a particularly stormy trip. I shared a tiny room in Mary's suite with her secretary, Kay Ulmar, she in the bottom berth and I in the top. In the middle of the night, both of us were sound asleep as the boat rounded Point Judith, a notoriously rough stretch at the mouth of Narragansett Bay. There was a sudden shudder and lurch and I found myself, fully awake, having fallen out of the bunk and into the tiny wash basin next to it. The following day I was covered with bruises caused by the sharp faucets. Mary, of course, slept soundly the whole night.

After the overnight voyage, passengers changed boats at New Bedford for the four or five hour trip to Nantucket with stops at Woods Hole and Oak Bluffs on Martha's Vineyard. Wrapped in her heavy English tweeds to withstand the raw June air, Mary sat on deck enjoying the salt spray, the wheeling sea gulls and the ship's motion. Once on the Island, Mary and her entourage put up at the Roberts House in Town for the 10 days it took to open Sunnycliffe for the summer. The caretaker removed the shutters from the windows, put down the boardwalk to the beach, and laid in a supply of coal for the kitchen stove and wood for the fireplaces. Dead birds and mice were fished out of the chimneys, the Florence stove received a new coat of blacking, salt was washed from the windows, furniture was uncovered, and doors flung open to get rid of winter's musty dampness. Mary hung fresh curtains, took newspapers off the books and thumbtacked new shelfpaper in all the drawers after removing the cloves that kept visiting silverfish at bay. She then went outdoors to plant her annuals, prune the hydrangeas and tie up the clematis that rambled up the trellises. Before anyone arrived, she had picked fresh bay leaves and broom to decorate and scent the rooms.

During the annual settling in period, Mary spend much of her time training cooks and waitresses, many of whom were neophytes, but glad for a job. With them she was both patient and demanding. She was an excellent hostess and to be one required a well-trained staff. Her spontaneous invitations to lunch or to tea often dismayed the cook or maids, and for some it was too much. Most, however, were loyal and hard-working.

There's no doubt, though, that Mary Oliver was impetuous and unpredictable, often acting on emotion rather than reason, but usually with great wit and *joie de vivre*. For some this was what made her so fascinating.

One year Mary fell in love with a little dog. She wanted to take him to Nantucket and asked her niece Katrina Leeb, who had a dog herself, if she would help her. Katrina, who found her aunt's whims delightful, agreed. When she arrived with her suitcase, she was greeted by Spike, a small, bouncy terrier. "Isn't he beautiful!" exclaimed Mary. Katrina wasn't so sure. Spike came from a kennel in New Jersey. Of dubious heritage, he was still quite young. Mary told Katrina that she had a tin of meat for Spike, enough for the two-day trip. But aboard the boat when it was time to feed Spike, Mary wasn't sure the meat was still fresh. She called the steward to her cabin and asked him to taste it. He refused politely, and hungry Spike gobbled it up. When they arrived at Sunnycliffe the next day, the dog happily romped in the coarse grass and chased butterflies. But soon Katrina and Mary noticed that he was not bouncing about. He was, in fact, quite lethargic. Was he sick? Had the meat gone bad? Mary didn't wait long to solve the problem. "Well," she said, "we'll just have to send him back to the kennel," which she did. Spike was crated up and sent to New Jersey, although Mary neglected to tell the kennel that he was coming. He arrived in sorry state and the kennel sued Mary for neglect. A trial in Trenton was scheduled to follow with Katrina to be called as a witness, but Mary's brother Lewie came to the rescue and succeeded in getting the case settled out of court. No one ever proved whether the meat was bad, if Spike was sick before he came to Mary, or if the trip back to the kennel did him in.

Mary dismissed all that in her mind and chose only to remember him as a lovely little dog.

One of Mary's nephews remembered his unpredictable aunt who came to visit his mother Alice and her family at Falmouth Foreside, Maine. Mary learned that a family of harbor seals lived in a cave near the house and asked her surprised nephew to row her out to see them. She told him that seals were fond of music and she planned to sing for them. As they approached the cave entrance, the seals, sprawled about on the kelp-covered rocks, looked up with interest. Mary stood up in the boat and broke into a soulful rendition of "Santa Lucia." No sooner had she begun than the startled mammals wriggled into the water, never to be seen again. Forsaking her original premise, she told everyone for years afterwards that she had proved that seals had no taste for music.

In 1931, Mary developed diabetes — too much bread and potatoes, she was told — and spent several months at the Joslin Clinic in Boston while doctors determined how to manage her disease. She hated the diet restrictions, the daily injections of insulin, and the watchful nurses who cared for her. Once she bribed a maid to bring her a box of chocolates which she ate when the nurse wasn't around and promptly went into a diabetic coma. Gradually, as a result of diabetes, she lost her eyesight during the last years of her life. Being legally blind made her eligible for a Seeing Eye dog. Undampened by her experience with Spike, Mary learned how to work with the dogs which were specially trained in Morristown, New Jersey, not far from East Orange. When Mary and her first dog arrived in Sconset, my nine-year old brother Teddy was fascinated. He tied a blindfold over his eyes and tried to get the dog to lead him around. The dog was trained, however, only to obey Mary and just lay on the front lawn watching the bunnies which nibbled the grass around Sunnycliffe.

Mary met change with fortitude and faith in God's will, but not always with grace. When she could shape life to suit her, she was the charming, witty hostess, the loyal friend, the loving sister/mother/grandmother. She was the patron of beauty, of art, of romance whose zest for life and spontaneous, unplanned adventures, kept everyone intrigued and amused. But when the world she desired changed or fell apart, she became querulous, demanding, short-tempered and difficult. With time, those who loved her chose to remember her charm, her whimsical ways, her talents and her deeply loving and loyal nature.

# Chapter Eight
# Duty Before Pleasure

*Norris Schermerhorn
Oliver, 5 yrs. old—1894*

On the surface of it, "duty before pleasure" epitomizes virtue and saintliness. But to live one's life under the burden of such a dictum becomes martyrdom, and for Norris Schermerhorn Oliver it was an integral part of his character.

Norris, named for his father's best friend in medical school, George Norris, was born May 19, 1888. He inherited his Spanish grandmother's dark hair, olive skin, deep brown eyes, and aquiline features. Even as a child he looked serious and somewhat morose. While the Olivers lived in Philadelphia Norris attended Episcopal Academy, did his schoolwork dutifully and studied the violin. He adored his father and wanted more than anything to be a doctor, and he shared his mother's love of music and reading.

Norris was 14 when his parents separated and the trauma left him with an unrequited love for the father who was gone. Mary's sister, practical-minded Alice Carter decided that boarding school was the answer. How easy it was in those days. She wrote to her dear friend, Dr. Edward Dudley Tibbetts, Headmaster of the Hoosac School in New York state who arranged a scholarship and shortly afterwards welcomed Norris as a student. Alice also reasoned that she could keep an eye on her nephew from nearby Williamstown and include him in family weekends. Norris graduated from Hoosac in 1908 and was accepted at Williams where he had two happy years, made lifelong friends, and joined Delta Psi fraternity to which he was fiercely loyal all his life. In the back of his mind, however, was the persistent desire to become a doctor.

At the end of sophomore year, Norris left Williams for Physicians and Surgeons medical school in New York City, with a letter in his pocket from Williams' president, Dr. Harry Garfield, saying that he could return to college at any time and graduate with any class. But fate intervened with a pink eye epidemic. In those days, without antibiotics, the infection was serious and Norris was left with weakened eyes. "I'm sorry, young man," said his doctor, "but a career in medicine is not possible; there is too much reading and close work." Norris was shattered, but set his mind to finding another career.

That summer he joined Dr. Wilfred Grenfell's medical mission to Newfoundland and Labrador aboard the *Strathcona*. Dr. Grenfell was a close friend of the Olivers and most willing to take on a young assistant. The ship stopped at small coastal settlements to bring medical supplies, deliver babies and perform surgery. For Norris, it was an exhilarating experience. The next year brought an opportunity to sail around South America while tutoring the son of an Army General. The boy had been sick but was determined to make up the work necessary for college acceptance. Years later Norris would recall with pleasure his trip around Cape Horn, a feat that qualified him for membership in Nantucket's exclusive Pacific Club, all of whose members had rounded the fearful Cape.

Back from South America, Norris tried his hand in his Uncle Lewie's sugar brokerage, sold paper for a brief period for the Canfield Paper Company, and finally found a job selling stocks and bonds for the Morgan Guaranty Company in New York. The last was a good choice of careers, for it entailed telephoning most of the day rather than reading. Eventually, Norris took his own list of clients to a desk at Kidder, Peabody & Company where he stayed for 30 years. He was scrupulously honest, conservative, and conscientious, and the only problem was that, although he became very good at it, Norris never really liked selling stocks and bonds.

During World War I, Norris served with the Army. In only 22 months, he rose from First Lieutenant to Major in the Infantry. But, to his disappointment, he found himself not in a trench in France, but in Plattsburg, New York as an instructor at an Officer's Training Camp. Even with the title of Commanding Officer of a battalion, it wasn't a glamorous job. Each week he sent his pay cheque to his mother, Mary, with instructions to buy privet bushes for Sunnycliffe. In time, these little plants, pampered by Nantucket's benign climate, grew to surround the property. In my childhood a solid line of six-foot high privet hedge protected the house.

*Capt. Norris S. Oliver, an Infantry instructor during WWI*

Early in his life, Norris developed a strong sense of family. Not only did he feel responsible for his mother's welfare and happiness, but he felt a duty to provide for generations to come.

He never married because, as he told his sister, "I could never find a long-necked, red-haired Philadelphia girl of impeccable origin." No doubt his Uncle Lewie's auburn-haired wife Margaret made a profound impression on then 22- year-old Norris. The one time he was ready to succumb, his fiancée broke off the engagement to become an Episcopal nun. His ambitions thus became focussed on insuring his family's financial independence. And this meant denying himself anything but the necessities of life. He made a lifelong study of his family, tracing his ancestry through historical societies, town records and correspondence with scattered relatives. He spent weekends examining worn slate gravestones in Pennsylvania and New York State cemeteries, trying to put the pieces of family history into place. On the first page of the "Book of Origins" that he spent his life compiling, he quoted Plutarch: "It is indeed a desirable thing to be well-descended, but the glory belongs to our ancestors." And although he yearned to visit La Coruña in Spain where the Suarez family came from (and he could have easily afforded it), he never allowed himself this personal indulgence. He might have traveled to Exeter, England, from where Nicholas Oliver, with his Bible and two other books in hand, emigrated to Philadelphia with his aunt in 1760. But Norris never did.

Instead he poured love into Sunnycliffe, the solid, well-rooted, dependable house that never let him down for 74 years.

My memories of Norris date from the mid-1930s. By that time his mother Mary had lost her eyesight and Norris took over much of her care. Although her brother Lewie helped financially and provided surprise treats, Norris accepted the major responsibility for her throughout the year. He read to her, took her to church and for Sunday drives, and interviewed and hired the nurses and secretaries who became increasingly necessary. Given his obsession for conservative money management, he worried about the expenses of running houses at East Orange and at Sconset. Mary didn't understand money, but Norris never criticized her. Instead he tried to cut expenses by doing minor repairs and painting himself.

Norris came to the Island for the Fourth of July by way of the overnight Cape Codder, the train from New York to Woods Hole, and by steamer to Nantucket. He always arrived pale and exhausted, in his three-piece, brown tweed, Brooks Brothers suit, white shirt, brown, knitted necktie, and round-toed, brown Brooks Brothers shoes. The moment he reached Sunnycliffe, he shed his city clothes for bathing trunks and went to the beach.

To us children who had not been allowed in the water in June, that meant it was finally warm enough for swimming. Norris returned to New York for July, but always arrived on the first of August for his month's vacation. Most days, after breakfast on the front porch, my brother and I joined Norris for his ritual walk up the Bluff to Sankaty Light. He always stopped to chat with the neighbors: elderly, deaf Anne Wilson, Miss Wilmerding in "Flagship", Mrs. Eichelberger and her daughter Jane, and the French teachers from Wellesley, Mlles. Heubner and Rueche. Sometimes he chatted with Stanley Swift, one of Uncle Lewie's golfing friends. My brother recalls that Stanley Swift "had a small black and white Boston terrier who had learned to find and retrieve golf balls. Mr. Swift carried a large empty pail to the Sankaty Head Golf Club, and while he played, the dog dashed hither and yon collecting balls that soon filled the pail."

Swimming followed the walk. A great advocate of physical fitness, Norris swam a mile a day with the current, either up to Sankaty or down to the Village. He walked back at the surf's edge and lay in the sun, absorbing Vitamin D and acquiring a deep tan that, in the 1930s and 1940s was considered a sign of good health. I swam with him somewhat reluctantly because I was thin and got quite cold in our long float. Some days the water was "dirty", that is it was full of reddish-brown, prickly seaweed that worked its way into bathing suits and was quite disagreeable to swim through.

*Norris Oliver with Teddy and Kay on Sconset Beach—1935*

After lunch (usually a sandwich because Norris loved bread), he settled down on the porch off the guest room for an hour's reading of his favorite authors; Trollope, Thackeray, Cervantes, Jack London and George Santayana. For most of his life he refused to wear glasses, claiming that his eyes became stronger without them.

The rest of the afternoon was devoted to house work. Although I think he really enjoyed scraping paint, puttying windows and doing minor carpentry, these were both money-savers and Norris's way of sharing in Sunnycliffe's upkeep. He considered it unsuitable for a man to do domestic chores, however, with two exceptions. He was very proud of his Brooks Brothers "wash and wear" shirts which he laundered himself, and he washed the dinner dishes each night. Unfortunately, the light in the kitchen was so poor that he often missed bits of food on the plates. We took perverse delight in calling out "Reject!" and giving him back the dirty dish.

The job closest to Norris' heart was maintaining the privet hedge. Each year he attacked the hedge with his hand clippers, standing on a wooden step ladder. It took him nearly a week because he tried hard, and usually unsuccessfully, to trim the top evenly. But the hedge was his personal triumph. More successful, was the yearly battle he fought and won with poison ivy that choked the boardwalk leading to the beach. Norris applied weed killer with a large kitchen spoon and then nailed up a sign warning us not to use the path for 24 hours. Eventually the poison ivy withered and died, but each year it invaded the boardwalk with fresh vigor. Once a summer Norris posted another sign, "Private Property" to insure our beach rights. According to Town law, the public was allowed to walk along the Bluff from the Village to Sankaty across homeowners' property, and they were permitted to walk the beach. But access to the beach was only allowed on public ways. The statute was legally binding if homeowners posted their steps annually. Nowadays, walking the Bluff is prohibited because erosion, particularly near Sankaty Light, has made the path dangerous. One homeowner, Dr. Karl Landsteiner, who lived near the Light, disliked having the public cross his lawn. To discourage them, he trained his two sprinklers on the passing walkers so that it was almost impossible not to get drenched. We didn't know him, but behind his back called him Professor Water Schnozzle. Only much later did we learn that he had won the Nobel Prize in 1930 for discovering the four blood types, and isolating the Rh factor in human blood.

Norris refused to go to Island parties because he felt he couldn't repay his hosts. He spent most of his vacation at Sunnycliffe except for an occasional evening when he walked down the Bluff to visit his friend Ray Hanlon, or Malcolm MacArthur (a cousin of General Douglas MacArthur's). Once in a while he walked to the Village to see a movie at the Casino.

*Planting Norris' privet hedge at Sunnycliffe— 1917*

Many nights, however, he stretched out on the sofa in Sunnycliffe's living room and listened to my mother play the piano. His only indulgence was fishing. Off-Island, Norris fished in the Pompton Lakes in western New Jersey, and at Nantucket he loved surf-casting for bluefish off the beach, or fresh-water fishing in Gibbs Pond. The occasional pickerel that he caught were delicious if bony, but he seldom brought home a bluefish. He took meticulous care of his equipment at the end of each summer; oiled his rods, packed them in cotton flannel and locked everything in the wooden window seat of Lewie and Margaret's room that became his. Rubber hip boots, old pants, and jackets waited out the winter in his closet, and the room always had a musty, salt water smell.

Clubs took the place of close family ties in Norris's life. He enjoyed his affiliations with his fraternity, Delta Psi, the Williams Club in New York, the St. Nicholas Society for descendants of original Dutch settlers, and various other organizations that attested to his ancestors' participation and leadership in the country's wars. And Norris was loyal to friends and family throughout the year. One of his best friends was Head of the Order of the Holy Cross, an Episcopal monastery located on the Hudson River, with whom Norris kept in close touch. He visited his aunts and uncles, cousins, nieces and nephews, and wrote regularly to his sister, my mother, throughout his life. Many of these letters included genealogical details from his research that he felt she should have (these bored her) or instructions on how to save money (these maddened her). He had an almost pathological dread of running out of money which led him to buy only what he needed and invest the rest for the use of future generations.

Laudable as this trait seems, it overrode any spontaneity and joyfulness. Norris seldom let himself go or let anyone know that life could be happy. He was quiet, contemplative and introverted. He never quite lost the profound sadness that colored his world — the missed chances, the unfulfilled dreams, the unrequited love. Another side of his personality is seen less charitably. Norris had almost irrational religious, racial and social prejudices. He disliked Catholics, in spite of his Spanish grandmother, mistrusted Jews and, I suspect, anyone not born of what he thought of as a "good family." To Norris that meant one whose ancestors were originally from England, preferably from noble stock, who were well-educated, had chosen professions rather than trades, and were Protestants, preferably Episcopalians. If they had money, they didn't talk about it or flaunt it. If they didn't have money, they made do with serenity and ingenuity. They were always ladies and gentlemen. He did business with people from all walks of life, but was careful not to see them socially nor introduce them to his family. Before his sister married, he passed judgment and often cautioned her against particular male friends whom he considered unsuitable. Saddest of all, when he was dying of leukemia in 1961, he resisted having a blood transfusion for fear the donor might be black. When he finally agreed, it was too late.

Brought up to be proud of his ancestry, then knocked down by his parents' separation, sent to school on a scholarship, forced to live on charity, denied the one career he desired and the one woman he loved, it is understandable that this proud man turned away from personal happiness to avoid further disappointment. He turned instead to caring for his mother and making provision for future generations. He was intelligent, handsome, often witty and possessed of the best Christian virtues. "Duty before pleasure" was the cross he carried. And it was a heavy load that prevented him from enjoying life as much as he should have.

# Chapter Nine
## Katharine

Katharine Powell Oliver, born in 1892, spent her childhood summers in the Nursery of Sunnycliffe. George Gibbs, in building the house, must have anticipated Oliver children to come, for he built this room directly over the kitchen so that the heat from the black Florence stove warmed it and dried it out. With only two fireplaces in the whole house, Sunnycliffe could be cold and damp. As the fog rolled in, it seeped under window sills, through the pine walls and settled with clammy moistness at night between sheets and wool blankets. But in the Nursery, the babies would be cozy on chilly nights. In the room was a white painted bureau, a flat-topped wood desk, a wicker rocking chair and a dainty Franklin stove set between two closets at the western end. One closet was Katharine's and the other was for linen. On the floor of all the bedrooms were Persian wool or cotton rag rugs that the maids shook out daily for no matter how many times children were told to wash their feet when they came up from the beach, they tracked sand into the house.

Katharine was four years younger than Norris and was immediately cherished by her mother, Mary. In what must be

*Katharine Powell Oliver at 1 yr. old*

her first formal picture, she sits on a table, naked except for the suggestion of a diaper, waist deep in wild roses. One chubby knee and one foot peek out. She must have been about one and a half, with dark shoulder-length hair, bangs nearly touching her eyebrows, an oval pale face, tiny down-drawn mouth, straight nose and solemn eyes.

Childhood in Philadelphia was calm and predictable. The routine never varied for Katharine: breakfast with her parents, Miss Ritter's school, home for lunch, a nap, and an afternoon of roller-skating and tag with friends in Rittenhouse Square. Nursery tea followed "with my own silver mug and porringer" and was invariably milk, hot oatmeal (which she'd already been given for breakfast), bread and butter and fruit, usually stewed prunes or apricots. Once in a while there was a most exotic treat, a fresh pear or banana. On Sundays, Katharine went to Sunday School and church when she was old enough, and on those evenings when her father and his friends played music in the parlor, she and Norris sat at the top of the stairs to listen. Once, she remembered, the butler Sylvanus Johnson, brought the children raw oysters and petits fours as a special treat.

*Katharine Powell Oliver, 2 yrs. old*

Occasionally there were weekends in the country or Atlantic City, but otherwise, as she wrote, "At the most, in our peaceful house on Locust Street, we expected music, books, trips to the country, good private schools, suitable marriages and many, many hours of church worship and volunteer help for others."

When her parents separated in 1904, Katharine's world fell apart. Although not as attached to her father as Norris was, Katharine, at 12, was sensitive and romantic and felt the despair and shame of the situation. One day she was in Philadelphia, and the next she was in a tiny, hot, third-floor room at her grandmother's house at East Orange, New Jersey. She couldn't understand what had happened, and nobody explained. Her mother lay on a chaise-longue weeping, her relatives were silent, and no one spoke of her father.

There was, however, the promise and comfort of Nantucket summers, with aunts, uncles and cousins turning up for visits, and the whole island to enjoy. In particular, it was fun to be in Sconset.

The transition from fishing village to summer resort and artist colony took less than 50 years. The change might not have taken place but for the advertising acumen of Edward F.

Underhill. He reasoned, in the 1890's that he had tripped over a good thing — Siasconset with its pure, cool sea air — could provide a profitable business. He built three streets of little houses, exact replicas of the fishermen's houses on Main Street, which he understandably named the Underhill Cottages. Many are still there on Pochick, Evelyn and Lily Streets, albeit enlarged to suit their present owners.

Simple, inexpensive and aesthetically appealing, the cottages attracted a few writers and artists from Boston. Soon praise for Sconset's charms reached the theatrical community in New York, and hot, tired actors and actresses whose plays had closed for the summer in those pre-airconditioned days, packed up for a welcome vacation on the Island. Some lived at the Ocean View Hotel just south of the village square, or rented Mr. Underhill's little cottages. Eventually many built their own houses. They renamed Main Street Broadway. The sunned and swam at the main bathing beach, played bridge and golf, danced, sang, and put on impromptu plays and musicals. Seasoned cottagers watched their antics with quiet disapproval, and for some time Mary refused to allow Katharine to play with the daughters of the "stage folk." When she found out they were not only harmless but fun, she relented. They invigorated the social scene in the village as it had never been before.

The only community center that existed in Sconset before 1900 was the railroad station. Located just south of the village below bank, it boasted a room large enough for social gatherings. When a party was to be held, Oscar Folger, the expressman, brought a borrowed piano down to the station and hung Japanese lanterns about that transformed the depot into a ballroom. The station master played the violin!

In 1892, Mrs. Emily Rice of Detroit donated land and $800 was raised to build a Casino. By 1899, a stock company called the Siasconset Casino Association was formed and, in mid-July of 1900, an informal opening introduced excited residents to the beautiful gray-shingled building with its two tennis courts. In the evening the Casino was aglow with lamps and lanterns, local ladies took turns at the piano, and young and old joined in the Virginia Reel. Some people even went home, took a nap, changed their clothes and returned to dance. That August 4, crowds gathered again for the first Casino entertainment, an evening of musical selections, short skits and recitations. Each summer thereafter, dances were held weekly and during the day, serious domino and whist matches took place between the ladies of Sconset and Nantucket.

Music, actors, actresses, drama all appealed to Katharine who had shown an early musical talent that blossomed with piano lessons. By the time she moved back to East Orange to live, she had progressed through four books of Czerny exercises and could play all the Chopin preludes. One of her best childhood friends, Margaret Fawcett, was equally attracted to the world of music and theater.

Margaret's mother, whose stage name was Percy Haswell, was a beautiful and noted Shakespearean actress on the New York stage who toured with Otis Skinner and went on to make films, both silent and talking. Margaret's father, George Fawcett, acted in Maude Adams' company. The Fawcetts, who led the theatrical parade to the Island, raved about Sconset and were soon joined by friends: Frank Gillmore, Regan Hughston, Frank Craven, the Penroses from Baltimore, and Mrs. G. H. Gilbert (known as "Grandma" Gilbert) who joined the Repertory Company in New York City in her seventies. Another summer visitor was DeWolf Hopper, a leading singer in Gilbert & Sullivan operettas, but best known for his unique rendition of "Casey-At-The-Bat". Undoubtedly, the most famous summer visitor was "Queen of the Stage" Lillian Russell, who, after she retired and was married to Alexander Moore, came to Sconset to see her theater friends. Margaret Fawcett described her visit in her book *Sconset Heyday*: "On a bright Sconset afternoon, this kindly, glamorous lady with the wavy gold hair and hourglass figure was driven in a surrey out to the Sconset Golf Club . . . she wore a large black straw hat, tailored white blouse with high collar and a long black skirt, the outfit made fashionable by the Gibson Girl drawings of the era."

Young Margaret Fawcett and her friends, not to be outdone by the adults, decided to stage their own musicals. In 1904, Margaret wrote "Queen Nasturtium" and 12-year old Katharine Oliver was thrilled to play the musical accompaniment when composer-pianist Roy Webb was called away at the last moment. Roy and his brother Kenneth the lyricist, were well known for their musical hits and went on to have successful artistic careers. Roy wrote music for Hollywood movies in the 1930's, and Kenneth became a New York advertising man and author of *Cavalcade of America*.

Margaret Fawcett had no problem casting herself as Queen Nasturtium. Her younger sister Ruth and other Sconset girls were her ladies-in-waiting, each one a different flower. The New York actors and actresses taught the children to act and dance, and the local newspaper, the *Inquirer and Mirror* printed announcements and the program. Can't you picture the scene?

Nervous, shivering children, too excited to eat supper, stood in the wings as the performance started promptly at 7:45 p.m. Katharine Oliver, in high-necked white lawn dress, her dark hair tied back with a huge black ribbon, sat at the piano. She worried that she might make a mistake, but once she started she was fine, plunging into the Overture, a medley of Roy and Kenneth Webb tunes. The lights dimmed and the green baize curtains parted to reveal Queen Nasturtium and her tiny court of quivering flowers. Loud applause from the audience. The plot was simple and featured flower tableaux, a solo dance, the Japonica by Natalie Brush, and the appearance of the only boy, John Ehrisman. When the curtain went down, the audience cheered with happy approval, proud parents rushed to hug their dazed children, and steered them into the Green Room for lemonade, homemade cookies and penuche fudge.

The evening was such a success that Margaret was encouraged to write "A Day In Fairyland" for the next summer. It earned $40 that the children donated to the Hospital for Crippled Children in New York. In 1906, the summer thespians produced a "Vaudeville Performance" which featured two, one-act plays, a solo Spanish dance performed by Margaret Fawcett, and stunts by Fred Noyes Drake. But the evening belonged to Margaret's mother, Percy Haswell who sang Roy and Kenneth Webb's hit song, "My Siasconset Maid" accompanied by three awe-struck nineteen year olds, Tom Galvin, Arthur Hargrave and Norris Oliver.

Musicals and summer theater continued to be popular at the Casino, reaching a crescendo with a week-long Carnival in 1911. Masquerades, revues, children's parties, all planned and produced in the tiny summer colony, provided the social entertainment of the summer. The cohesive camaraderie, however, changed with the introduction of motion picture films. The Board of Selectmen granted the Casino Association a permit to show movies in July, 1915, and the era of creative homemade theatricals started to fade. But what fun Katharine and her friends had during those years.

Most of the time, however, Katharine and Norris spent their childhood summers close to Sunnycliffe. Sometimes they constructed boats out of wooden crates, sticks of wood and bed sheets, and "sailed" around the back yard. They swam, built sand castles and dug their way to China on their own beach in

*Katharine Oliver at the Bluff edge—10 yrs. old*

*Sankaty Light*

front of the house. And almost every evening they walked up the Bluff to see Mr. Larsen at Sankaty Light. The stocky, white-washed lighthouse with its belt of red was built in 1849 at a cost of $20,333 on the highest point of land on the Island, in direct line with Davis South Shoals to the southeast. These shoals, with their treacherous shifting sand, had claimed many a sailing ship, and Sankaty's light, the most powerful one on the coast at the time, flashed its warning for seven miles. The light contained the most modern Fresnel lens set in a prismed lantern that turned with weights, much like a grandfather clock. Mr. Larsen, the lighthouse keeper, lived with his family in an adjoining red-roofed house. Every evening, with Katharine and Norris following him, he climbed the steep, spiral iron grid steps, 166 feet above sea level to wind the chain for the weights, pour kerosene in the pan and light the wick. Around the outside of the light was a small iron-railed balcony. "Even when it was very windy," Katharine recalled, "he let us go out on the ledge alone while he lit the light just at the exact moment the sun was last seen above the western horizon."

Other times the two children walked down to the village to buy fish from Mr. Cash, who they called "Mr. Fish, the cashman." Fresh from the ocean, the fish were laid out on a bed of wet seaweed in the back of Mr. Cash's open cart. Thirty cents bought a whole haddock, cod or bluefish. Sometimes he would have a swordfish which he'd sell for forty cents.

Sunday, as in East Orange, was devoted to religion with Sunday school and church. After the service in the white clapboard Sconset Chapel, everyone, including the minister whom Mary always invited, went back to Sunnycliffe for a formal, sit-down lunch. Life flowed along with calm predictability.

The most important person in Katharine's life was her mother. Had Charles Oliver remained in the picture things might have been different. But Mary and Katharine needed each other and were inseparable. In Katharine, her mother found a kindred spirit, a girl who loved beauty, art, music and had a sensitive and romantic temperament. When she had to be away, Mary left little notes tucked under Katharine's pillow, pretty postcards or just a thought written on a scrap of paper. Katharine composed little poems to accompany presents, or picked wild flowers which she left for her mother to find on her bedside table. And Mary saved every message, memento and letter that Katharine ever wrote to her. After her death in 1938 Norris found a penciled letter that Katharine left for her mother when she was married in 1922. In it, Katharine, with tears streaming down her cheeks, writes that she can't bear being away from Mary, that while she loves her husband as man and wife, she has always loved her mother most of all — "I always have and I always will. I have tried so hard," she says, "to make up to you some of the things you have missed. You should have had just the loving kind of a husband that I am going to have." A bit further on, "And for 30 years you have always loved me, and helped me, and understood me when no one else could. I can never thank you for all you've done — but you have been everything to me always — and there never in the history of the world has been so unselfish and loving and kind a mother." Surely it was a combination of this love, compassion and sense of duty, revealed in that letter, that led Katharine to spend four months each year on Nantucket with Mary. But that was much later.

There were many things to occupy Katharine's young mind during her childhood. In September the real world of school began in East Orange. Katharine liked school, particularly English. Her marks in literature and composition were high, and she wrote with imagination in a lively style. At the same time she loved music, sang in the choir with her mother and played hymns for the family services. Early on she began to face to the dilemma that would plague her for a lifetime — music or writing?

Several important things happened when Katharine was 16. On her birthday in 1908, her uncle Lewie surprised her with the gift of a Steinway grand piano. She promptly announced her readiness to teach, although she wrote years later, "My past experience did not train me as a teacher, but that was not thought important in those days. You passed on what you knew — the scales, the basic chords, how to read the bass clef (always the hardest) and the 'Touch'. Besides, the Diller-Quaile teaching books had appeared and if you could read, you could teach. And so I did, with my lovely new piano, at home, for 50 cents an hour."

*Katharine Oliver at 16 yrs.*

That same spring, her guardian, Dr. James Thorington, invited her to spend a day with him in Philadelphia. She described it in her autobiography. "I took an early train over from Newark, in fear and trembling," she wrote, "for I had no idea why he wanted to see me. It turned out that he wanted me to know what a brilliant and scholarly man my father had been, and to show me where I had lived. The house was about to be torn down, my father lived in California, and this might be my only chance to learn something of my background.

"We went through 1507 Locust Street which suddenly looked tiny to me, and he took me to lunch at Bookbinder's restaurant. We walked by the Academy of Music and the Episcopal Academy, and then we went out to the University of Pennsylvania. I almost fainted with restored confidence and pride when I saw my father's portrait on the wall of the Medical School, and those of my grandfather and great-grandfather. It was a wonderful day and no one ever did a kinder thing. At last I could understand my mother's sadness and remorse and try to help her."

Later that year Katharine legally changed her middle name from Powell (on her father's side) to Schermerhorn. Glad to know about her father, it seems she was happier to carry the ancestral Dutch middle name of her mother's family.

Katharine was a serious and bright student who needed more of a challenge than the local school provided. Alice Carter, once again, had the answer. She knew the headmistress of nearby Miss Hall's School in Pittsfield, Massachusetts, and arranged for Katharine to have a scholarship. Alice's only daughter, Sallie, was at Miss Hall's and both Alice and Mary wanted the cousins to become good friends. It should have been a perfect solution, but, of course, it wasn't!  From the start, Katharine hated the school, and in particular the headmistress, Myra Hall, a formidable spinster with pewter-gray hair and steel-rimmed glasses.

At the first school assembly, Miss Hall announced in a clear voice, to Katharine's acute embarrassment: "Miss Oliver is our new scholarship student. In return for the privilege of an education here, she will play all the hymns for daily chapel and our two Sunday church services." Being thus singled out separated Katharine completely from her fashionable, rich East Coast classmates, most of whom would never pursue their education after Miss Hall's. She made up her mind to excel in the way most of her classmates didn't — in academics. Determination paid off in senior year when she passed the entrance examinations for Vassar, and became the first girl in the family to go to college.

# Chapter Ten
# All Those New
# Inventions

As the nineteenth century drew to a close Nantucket was still a far-away island, both physically and in point of view. Rooted in the customs of the past, islanders lived simple but worthwhile lives, paying little attention to the mainland except for the necessities that came by boat. It was the summer visitors from urban areas who insisted on having the amenities of their other world transported to the island, often at vast expense. Some of these conveniences took an even longer time to reach Sunnycliffe.

One was running water. By 1900, Mary Oliver felt she should live on Nantucket as she did in Philadelphia. She knew also that running water and flush toilets would give her an advantage in hiring servants for the summer. Most important probably was the real panic everyone had about typhoid fever which had reached epidemic proportions during the 1890s. Nantucket boasted of its clean, pure water and the Olivers were eager to have their own.

Thomas Clifton was called upon to find water at Sunnycliffe. When he did, a well was built off the northeast side of the house. First, a four-foot wide hole was drilled in the ground, not very deep because the water-bearing stratum lay near the surface. Next a brick casing was set in place to line the well with open pores left at certain spots to allow water to enter. The hole was covered and a wooden scaffold built over the well with a pipe leading from the well to the overhead feed tank. Windmill vanes turned to draw the water up to the tank and gravity pulled it down into the house through new piping. Later an electric pump controlled the water's flow. Once inside the house, water for cooking, washing and bathing was stored in a large cylinder attached to the Florence stove.

*Thomas Clifton—1900*

Until 1929, the family used one bathroom on the second floor next to the Nursery. The bathtub was an elegant, deep

oval that rested on ball and claw feet. Next to it the "water closet" had an overhead water tank and pull chain. Even when
there were three baths in Sunnycliffe and modern toilets had
replaced the water closets, the water in the toilet would rise up
and down in a severe storm. Across from the small, white sink
with its nickel-plated faucets was a full length mirror flanked
by a shallow medicine closet full of the patent remedies of the
day, liniments, cascara segrata (a laxative), oil of cloves for
toothache, tonics, foot powder and witch hazel for cuts and
bruises.

Mary Oliver viewed the bathroom not only as functional,
but as a quiet spot for personal reflection and inspiration. It was
also the place to which family members retreated to discuss the
most secret worries, plans and dreams. In both the family bath
and in Mary's later on, she tacked up a poem within easy view
of anyone who had the time to contemplate life.

> Look to this day,
> For it is life, the very life of life.
> In its brief course lie all the
> verities and realities of your existence;
> the bliss of growth, the glory of action,
> the splendor of beauty.
> For yesterday is but a dream and
> tomorrow is only a vision,
> but today well lived makes every yesterday
> a dream of happiness
> and every tomorrow a vision of hope.
> Look well, therefore, to this day.
> Such is the salutation of the dawn.

THE SUFI, 1200 BC (from the Sanskrit)

Mary loved the poem for its optimistic and romantic vision
of the good life. But at Sunnycliffe, with its diverse and idiosyn-
cratic residents trying to live together, the dream was seldom
realized. Instead, petty disagreements became major confronta-
tions, tempers flared, feelings were hurt and hopes dampened.
But, of course, it was ever thus throughout the world!

Mostly, there was great happiness at Sunnycliffe. Joy at the
freedom of space, the infinite horizon and the intimacy with out
of doors. Life slowed down to keep pace with the waves, breaking slowly and inevitably on the beach of Sankaty sand. Days
were long and lazy, punctuated only by the routine of meals.
What wasn't done today could be done tomorrow. Norris often

said that sitting on the second floor front porch looking out to sea refreshed him for a year.

For years everyone at Sunnycliffe took baths. Except, of course, my brother who often boasted that he hadn't taken a bath from June through August. What he didn't bother to say was that he spent most of every day swimming in salt water. Sunnycliffe women were more fastidious because, although they swam every day, they preferred the feeling of skin and hair washed in fresh water. Neither Mary, her contemporaries nor my mother Katharine washed their own hair. They had permanents that required professional help. Weekly appointments in Town were the rule until after World War II when Katharine discovered blonde, Swedish Miss Elna in Sconset. Miss Elna's magic fingers massaged special oil into the scalp that promised to combat the effects of salt water. As good as she was as a hairdresser, her most attractive attribute was that she knew all the village gossip which she gladly shared with her customers. I'm sure that in 1956 our friends learned of Sunnycliffe's new shower from Miss Elna! The news wasn't that startling because showers were hardly unique, but rather because Sunnycliffe was so behind the times. That first shower consisted of a long steel tube and shower head fitted to the bathtub water pipes. At the top of the tube a circle of metal tubing held the white canvas curtain. Once you were inside the bathtub, surrounded by canvas, there was so little turning room that it was almost impossible to soap up and rinse off. But, it was a step in the right direction and lasted for years. Finally, towards the end of the 1960s, the tub was replaced with a stall shower, a bit tinny but big enough for a proper shower.

Still, one of my happiest memories was soaking sore muscles in a chin-high tub of hot water, contemplating the "bliss of growth, the glory of action and the splendor of beauty."

The arrival of the telephone at Nantucket was an historic event. Invented by Alexander Graham Bell in 1876, the concept took time to catch on. Two years later, the first telephone switchboard appeared in New Haven, Connecticut and attracted 21 subscribers. Gradually, local systems combined to form regional companies linked together by long distance circuits under the name of Atlantic Telephone and Telegraph Company. In 1896, Guglielmo Marconi, a young and unknown Italian inventor, took out the first patent for wireless telegraphy in England. By 1899, he had established communication between England and France, and transatlantic telegraphy followed in 1900. In 1901, the first commercial Marconi wireless station on the American Coast was built on Bunker Hill in Sconset, a remote location selected and sponsored by the *New York Herald*. It was there that young Matt Tierney, the operator on April 14, 1912, was astonished to receive the first distress signal from the sinking *Titanic*.

Sconset's first telephone system operated out of a small, shingled cottage in the middle of the village. The switchboard operator sat at a panel of switches — one for each telephone in town — inserted the answering plug into the caller's answering jack, and by operating the answering key, could talk with the caller. Irene Cash, granddaughter of Mr. Cash the fishman, was Sconset's telephone operator during the 1920's and 1930's. She had short, curly red hair, wore steel-rimmed glasses and knew everything about everyone in town. "Oh, Mrs. Oliver," she would say to Mary, "Dr. X. is off-Island today. Shall I ring Dr. Z. for you? He's in his office this morning." Or, if my grandmother hoped to reach a friend, Irene knew where to find her on the Island. As an intermediary between caller and receiver, she could prepare you for the call. "It's your brother, Mrs. Oliver, and he has some bad news." Irene interrupted chatters for important calls, often took messages when lines were busy and, at her most unprofessional, repeated all the town gossip. During Mary's later years when she was blind and couldn't write, Irene came to Sunnycliffe as her secretary. Her neat and legible handwriting was a vast improvement over Mary's slant-ed and often unreadable script.

During World War II when Irene Cash had retired and oper-ators were hard to find, my not-yet-drafted friends filled in. They worked willingly and felt they were contributing to the war effort. But, after the war the telephone became fully auto-mated and we lost forever the personal touch of the human operator.

In another area, Sconset proved to be a strategic location in World War II. It was selected as an outpost for a new and then most secret naval operation. The Long-Range Navigation System Headquarters, known to all of us as the LORAN Station, was set up behind barbed wire at Low Beach between Sconset and Tom Never's Head. We didn't know what lay behind the wire fence, so we assumed that it was some sort of protection from enemy attack, probably from German submarines.

So important was the telephone in Sconset that at Sunnycliffe Charles Oliver's medical office was transformed into the Telephone Room. It continued to be called that until

1976. In Charles' day, he saw eye patients in this small room across from the dining room off the hall that separated the living room from the kitchen. When he no longer came to the Island, Mary replaced the black leather examining chair with a day bed, substituted modern fiction for ophthalmology textbooks and gave the closet over to games, tennis rackets, golf clubs, pails, shovels, rain gear and the croquet set. Game parts that had lost their boxes were put into baskets along with dominoes, cards, game instructions and shuttlecocks. One basket contained hundreds of glass marbles, some with dark swirls — cat's eyes, and one that my oldest daughter remembers as "rough and blue-green with squiggles."

The baskets were unique. They were the original Nantucket Lightship baskets, made by the men whose long and uneventful days aboard the lightships gave them plenty of spare time. Unlike the durable farm baskets of ash, hickory and oak made throughout New England, lightship baskets were made of rattan. One unusual feature was a solid wood bottom into which the ribs were inserted in incised grooves. These bottoms were stronger than the woven, intricate spider-web ones of most farm baskets. Another unique characteristic of Nantucket baskets was that they were made on wooden molds, often fashioned from pieces of ships' masts. In Mary's day lightship baskets were for sale all over the Island and most families had plenty of them in all sizes. On the South Shoal Lightship, men made nests of baskets and my brother Teddy recalls that the only item stolen from Sunnycliffe during his youth was an original nested set, ranging from a basket that held a single egg to the largest that measured 21 and 1/2 inches across. Nowadays, an original nest is worth $20,000.

Basket-making on lightships stopped at the end of the the century, but the craft has continued on land. In 1948, José Formoso Reyes, a skilled craftsman from the Phillipines with a Harvard degree, living on Nantucket, made a small basket with a woven lid, to be used as a lady's handbag. Charlie Sayle, a master carpenter and fisherman who carved ivory and ebony whale pins as a hobby, shaped a small black whale for José who glued it to the wooden oval in the middle of the basket's lid and the modern Nantucket basket was born. Today, the tops are elaborate with carved flowers, mammals or birds in color or black and white scrimshaw. Customers can personalize their baskets with initials, maps or designs of their houses. Copies are for sale all over the world. The popularity of the handmade basket has raised the price astronomically, and sadly, the "Nantucket Lightship Basket" has become a status symbol. It's not unusual to see two well-to-do strangers in a foreign city fall on each other as if they were dear friends as they compare their authentic Nantucket baskets. But in the game closet of the Telephone Room at Sunnycliffe, the baskets were functional and sturdy.

One of the most controversial issues on Nantucket swirled around the arrival of the automobile. When Charles and Mary Oliver first drove around the Island it was along dusty, rutted dirt roads in a horse-drawn carriage. Or they rode in a "box wagon" with two seats, low chairs or even rockers taking the place of a back seat.

In 1881, through the efforts of Philip H. Folger, a Nantucket railroad company was formed and a narrow gauge line built. The first train, *Dionis* (named for the wife of one of Nantucket's first settlers, Tristram Coffin), went into service to carry passengers from the Steamship Wharf in Town to Surfside, considered by many to be the upcoming tourist mecca. By 1884, service was extended across the Island and a second train, *Sconset*, was added in 1885. Its terminus was a small station below the bank on the south side of the village.

Unfortunately, those who laid the original track hadn't reckoned with winter storms and heavy surf which washed away the railroad in Sconset in 1887, again in 1888, and in 1893 for a long stretch at Nobadeer on the South Shore. At that point the company realized it was fighting an uphill struggle with the elements and abandoned the three-mile run to Surfside. With the railroad's demise went all hope of Surfside's becoming a tourist attraction until much later in the century when swimmers came to appreciate its superior beach with its combers and rollers.

Without trains, islanders were forced to use a stage coach until 1905 when Cromwell G. and Thomas G. Macy brought a gasoline motor car called "The Bug" to Nantucket. It held six to eight passengers and its trailer, the "Birdcage," carried trunks. The owners announced with great pride that The Bug ran on the old train tracks, an economic advantage, and that the trip from Town to Sconset took just 19 minutes. The first run, greeted with immense anticipation, proved a disaster. The car died two miles outside of Town leaving all the passengers stuck in the pine woods. It was dark before some of the stronger men could push it back to Town. When The Bug was "debugged," operation resumed with two trips a day across the Island. The next year saw the appearance of a 30-passenger motor car, but it vibrated too much for most people's comfort. Luckily, a new line of track was laid for the train in 1909. Less luckily, the first locomotive turned over on the 23rd of July, but was righted and went on! In spite of new equipment — passenger and baggage cars and an infusion of New York money, the train company was a losing venture. In 1917, the rolling stock was sold for scrap iron that was used for armaments in World War I, and the Nantucket railroad was history. But, by then, most Nantucketers had automobiles.

As the train vanished, the automobile was finally legalized on the Island after years of argument and discontent. The first rumble of what was to be an explosive issue began in 1900. Nantucketer Arthur Folger and his son George brought a brand-new Stanley Steamer to the Island. They were followed by Samuel Howe of Ithaca, New York, the proud owner of a gas-powered Locomobile. Then on August 3, the Island newspaper observed that "a steam driven outfit owned by Mr. Howard Willets lumbered ashore." It was too much. The Island felt it had been invaded by noisy, belching dragons.

Protest against the invasion was so strong in 1907 that Selectmen passed an exclusion regulation, defied by some spunky Bostonians who drove their cars around the Island just to see who would stop them. After frightening the horses and townspeople, they were, indeed, stopped and taken to court. Sympathy for the islanders ran high on Beacon Hill and a bill was passed by the Legislature in April, 1908 that allowed Selectmen to ban automobiles on Nantucket from June 15 to September 15. It was fine until Clinton Folger brought his Overland touring car to the Island in November, 1913, determined to outwit the law.

Officially, cars were prohibited on the roads by a vote of 376 to 234 in a special Nantucket town meeting on June 18, 1914. But that spring Clinton Folger had won the mail contract between Nantucket and Sconset. With a wink to authority, Mr. Folger drove his Overland from Sconset to the first milestone outside of Town. There he hitched his car to a horse-drawn box wagon, turned off the engine, and let the horses pull him into Town. There he would sit, walrus-moustached Mr. Folger, arms crossed over his ample chest, looking solemn but self-satisfied in his "horsemobile." He was, technically, in compliance, but the selectmen threatened him, repassed the exclusion act and seethed. Mr. Folger, however, had the last word. He continued to deliver the mail and lent his car to doctors for emergency calls. Who would or could oppose helping the sick?

As long as Thomas Clifton worked for Mary Oliver, he provided his horse and carriage. His successor, in 1923, was Charlie Morris, the proud owner of a Buick, which, unfortunately, Mary found extremely uncomfortable to ride in. By 1925, automobiles were commonplace on Nantucket, thanks to the capacity of the steamer *Nobska*, which could carry 50 cars across Nantucket Sound on each trip. Lewie, always eager to join a new trend, was quick to bring his black Packard to the Island. Katharine, married and the mother of two children in 1928, brought her own car to the Island. A special Massachusetts summer driving license cost one dollar and soon the Island was clogged with cars, taxis and trucks. For a modest price, even tourists could bring their vehicles over for a day or two to tour the Island.

By the 1930s, getting to Nantucket was considerably easier than it had been. The night Cape Codder enabled businessmen to leave their offices Friday afternoon, board the train in New York City or at stops along the Connecticut and Rhode Island shore, connect with the early morning steamer from Woods Hole, and arrive at Nantucket around 11 on Saturday morning.

When my mother and father drove from Cleveland or Washington, they took the boat from New Bedford because they liked to spend the night at the New Bedford hotel. Its Whaler Bar replicated the inside of a whaling ship. The entrance was over a narrow gangplank of weathered, gray wood with shimmering blue light underneath to simulate water. The dining area was illuminated with ships' lanterns and through the portholes on the walls you could see painted scenes of sailors in their whale boats, harpoons poised, as a spouting whale emerged from the deep, breaking through the foaming waves. It was dramatic! And the seafood was delicious. A dinner there heightened the anticipation of reaching Nantucket.

The next morning my father maneuvered the car onto the Nantucket boat. It was no easy feat as the opening was on the side. He had to drive up the steep narrow ramp and, once aboard, taking directions from one of the crew, put the car into reverse and back into the assigned space, avoiding the steel bulkheads on either side. The trip took almost five hours with stops at Woods Hole and Oak Bluffs on Martha's Vineyard. After that the ship headed for the open ocean of Nantucket Sound. As children we explored the boat and sometimes sat on the top deck for the whole trip, arriving with a dreadful sunburn in those innocent days when we knew nothing about skin cancer. Sea gulls soared and dipped off the stern, swooping to catch bread that passengers threw at them. Half way across we rounded the bright red Nantucket lightship where, in earlier times, the boat dropped off mail and newspapers. Once we had turned at the lightship we started scanning the horizon for the first glimpse of the Island. On clear days we saw the tall, white shape of Great Point light on the left. Coming closer, we identified the gray cylinder of the Nantucket water tower. Suddenly, we were inside the stone jetties that form the channel into the harbor and torn between staying on deck until we docked or being in the car, ready to drive off. The steamer slowed, a shrill whistle sounded and we rounded Brant Point Light, white with its little black hat. At last the engines went into reverse and with aquamarine foam swirling around the stern, we came to a stop at the steamer dock, which the boat usually hit!

When I was 12 or 13, I made the trip from Nantucket to Washington by myself. My grandmother Mary Oliver knew the captain of the *Nantucket* and asked him as a special favor, to let me visit the bridge. The boat left at seven a.m. and this particular day dawned warm, sunny and absolutely clear, without a trace of the usual early morning fog. I will never forget looking out the window of the bridge, high up over the water and seeing, as we cleared the Jetties, Martha's Vineyard on the left and 30 miles away, Wood's Hole. From there to the tip of Cape Cod, the long flat line of the Cape was visible on the right.

Airplane service came to Nantucket in the 1930s. Lewie and Jay, of course, were among the first daring souls to commute regularly between New York and the Island. On one of those early flights, Lewie got off the plane at Nantucket, found his suitcase and walked away. He never looked back to see the plane he'd just left moments before burst into flames on the runway! Airplane travel wasn't easy, nor is it today. In spite of sophisticated electronic equipment, Nantucket fog still has the final word. Many nights at Sunnycliffe, a frustrated voice on the telephone would announce that he or she was stranded in Hyannis or Boston, and would be bussed to the next possible boat. Some visitors, when asked what they did on their weekend, said they spent most of their time figuring out how to get off the island.

Running water, the telephone, the automobile and the airplane were all inventions that eased life and made Nantucket seem nearer to the rest of the United States. For the Henrys and Olivers, the fruits of modern technology gave them freedom and more opportunities to see friends and to enjoy Island activities. With a telephone there was quick access to Ashley's Market in Town, to Mary's doctors, and to family and friends off Island. A car spelled independence and introduced people to other parts of Nantucket beyond their back yards. Perhaps, though, those early islanders who fought the automobile, and were reluctant to use the telephone and the airplane, were right in trying to maintain the innocence and purity of island life. The unique quality of Nantucket was lost, and in its place came the complexities and complications of transposing an urban life to an island setting. Many are happy with the changes, but some, I suspect, remember with wistful longing, those early, happy and simpler days.

# Chapter Eleven
## The Great War and After

Katharine went to Vassar in the fall of 1911 on a full scholarship for which she was eligible through her Henry ancestors. In the early nineteenth century, the Spingler Institute for Women flourished under the aegis of Arthur Spingler, a great friend of Matthew Vassar, the college's founding father. Both Mr. Spingler and Mr. Vassar believed in education for women and to this end established a scholarship at Vassar for graduates of the Spingler Institute. Nearly 100 years later, Katharine Oliver was awarded the Spingler scholarship as the only qualified descendant of a Spingler graduate for the year 1911.

Katharine was thrilled with every new experience. Her first roommate, Mary Mallon, opened her eyes to the greater world and guided her into "the mystery of politics, the principles of the Fabian Society, the poetry of Lesbos, Irish literary criticism and the Vassar Library with its huge collection of exciting books." Katharine majored in English and began to write seriously as a reporter for the literary magazine, *The Miscellany*. She remembered one time when the magazine's editorial board sent her off to tell a young poet that her poem had been rejected for publication. Katharine knocked on a door in Main Hall and entered to find a pale, thin girl with flame red hair lying on the bed. Katharine delivered the message with the gravity that behooved a cub reporter and the girl sat up, smiled and said: "That's all right, I've just received a cheque from the *North American Review* for the poem. It's called 'Renascence.'" The girl, of course, was Edna St. Vincent Millay. Known as Vincent at Vassar, she and Katharine later became good friends. Most of Katharine's college friends were budding writers or would be connected with the world of letters, and these mind-expanding years were very happy ones for her. She continued to study musical theory and composition; she played the piano and sang in the choir.

In 1914, at the end of her junior year at Vassar, her mother proposed a trip to Europe — a family tradition for girls before they found husbands and settled down. Katharine chose a col-

*Mary Henry Oliver and
Louisa Henry in 1927*

lege friend named Sylvie and Mary's sister Louisa made a
fourth. The group booked passage on a small Cunarder taking
the Mediterranean route and spent three leisurely weeks cross-
ing the Atlantic. The ship stopped at Madeira, Gibraltar, Algiers
and Patras before sailing up the Adriatic to Trieste and Fiume.
From there the foursome drove along the Italian Riviera to
Abbazia, an Austrian seaside resort, and then traveled by train
to Florence, Venice, Padua, Switzerland and France. Katharine
was enchanted with the beauty of Paris, its opera, parks, flowers, colors, and museums and could have stayed there forever.
But, Mary announced that they must see a little of Germany
where she had been on her wedding trip.

It was in the Schlöss Hotel in Heidelberg that they read
with horror that the Archduke Ferdinand had been murdered in
Sarejevo, Bosnia on June 28, and although the four women
knew nothing about it, the first world war had begun. Within
an hour, the hotel manager demanded they leave for England.
As neutrals, they would be able to travel to Strasbourg and
Holland. They packed, collected as much money as the manager could give them, and boarded the first train available. In the
evening of the first day, they were dozing when a railway offi-
cial came through the car and announced: "All foreigners get
out here!"

"Here", my mother wrote, "was a bleak, small railroad station on the border between Germany and France called
Deutsch-Auricourt." The 12 "foreigners" got off, and were
relieved of their tickets, passports, luggage and money by the
Germans. Other than the small bottle of blackberry brandy that
Mary always carried, they had nothing to eat or drink for the
next day and a half, except for some bread that a fellow traveler
shared with them. As troop trains rumbled through the station
all night, the blond German soldiers bound for the front waved
cheerfully to them. Finally, on the third evening, a train, headed
for the Hook of Holland, arrived with an empty car. Weak with
hunger and fear, the travellers hurried aboard, glad at last to be
on their way to safety. The train started out of the station but
suddenly jerked to a stop. Into their car strode an enormous
German officer, covered with medals and ribbons, and followed
by two aides carrying a small, square box. The officer's eye lit
on Louisa Henry, straight-backed and impeccably dressed, sitting next to Mary on the red plush seat. "Macht Aus!" he
ordered. Not one to be intimidated, Louisa drew herself up and
in a voice cold with rage, said… "I do not care if you are the
President of this railroad or the Kaiser, I do not intend to give
you my seat." The officer glared at her as his aides whipped out

their revolvers. Mary sensed a very real danger and rose slowly from her seat. "Take mine," she murmured. Thereupon the aides put back their guns and placed the square box on Mary's seat while she stood in the aisle.

None of them could take their eyes off the box and Katharine always said she was sure it contained dynamite. But they never knew as the Germans and the box left the train at Strasbourg. At 11:30 on the third night, the train reached the Hook of Holland where hundreds of refugees were waiting to board a boat for England. In a fierce rainstorm and lashed by a cold wind from the North Sea, they made their way to the dock. Katharine described the night: ". . . by now my mother and aunt were too ill to eat, and I doubted if I could get them on the boat. As so often happens in a real crisis, bystanders, strangers, simply help, and someone carried my mother inside the steamer where a woman who told me the next day she was a Christian Science healer, gave my mother her berth and sat beside her all night putting wet compresses on her feverish head. The crowds were so dense Sylvie and I never got further than the deck. In the pouring rain, with huge seas washing over us at intervals, we simply lay down, spoon-fashion, and took it. A handsome young Englishman, who we never met, took off his overcoat and tossed it over us. Destroyers throwing flares ahead (for the Channel had been mined), traveled each side of us. An old witch-like creature on the dock at the Hook had hissed at us: 'That boat will sink tonight.' It didn't but it was the last English ship to take refugees across the Channel before the war started."

The next day, on the boat train to London, a distinguished English lady, beautifully-dressed and holding a tiny white poodle, listened to their tale of horror and offered them money for train fare. They accepted gratefully and the following day when they arrived at her Grosvenor Square town house with a bunch of flowers and the money, their benefactress insisted that they stay for tea, served by two footmen. Katharine never forgot this unexpected and most welcome kindness.

Six weeks later, new passports arrived from the United States and the four women found berths on a small ship. Their terrified fellow passengers, insisting that the North Atlantic was full of German mines, scanned the horizon for enemy periscopes and moaned that the ship would be blown up. Mary was cheerful and assured her party: "If it is God's intent to blow up the ship, it surely will be done and there is no sense in worrying about it." God, it seemed, had other plans for the tiny boat for it reached New York three weeks later to discharge its happy and relieved passengers. It was one of the very few summers that Mary and Katharine failed to visit Nantucket.

In 1990, 85 years later, my husband and I also stopped at Hoek van Holland. There was the brownstone Romanesque station built in 1900, with train tracks leading back to Rotterdam, across Holland, into Germany. At the dock stood, not the last little ship to help refugees escape World War I, but the Princess Beatrix, an all-white, luxurious passenger steamer of the Stena Line, her red, white and blue flag ruffling in the wind. The day was bright and sunny, but I thought of the scene in 1914 and imagined the relief those travelers felt, knowing that Harwich, England was less than 24 hours away.

In the summers during World War I, the Henrys and Olivers still went to Nantucket. Lewie and Jay were in their forties and too old to enlist. Norris was training future Army officers in upper New York state. Mary and Katharine cultivated a "Victory Garden" that supplied them with vegetables, planted the privet bushes that Norris's pay cheques provided, and knitted khaki wool scarves and socks. Social life in Sconset understandably dwindled. The Casino, which had opened so proudly in 1900, was threatened with bankruptcy and was only kept afloat by a small group of benefactors. Yet, in spite of financial strictures, it kept its traditions as best it could. The summer opened with an early July party. Sunday night lecturers brought insight about the war. Occasional dances were held and always, the August children's masquerade took place, as it still does today.

In 1915, Katharine was graduated from Vassar with the first prize in music. It carried with it the honor of playing for the whole college on the Sunday night before commencement, and she chose the Mozart D Minor Concerto. All through college her dream had been to study music at the Paris Conservatoire, but her family opposed it. First of all, World War l made foreign travel impossible. Then, her usually generous Uncle Lewie refused financial help. Mary's reason was more personal. "You'll never find a suitable husband if you go off to Paris and live like a Bohemian."

Well, there were other ways to live the life she wanted, Bohemian or not. Unlike her Aunt Louisa who never questioned her parents' decision about her life, Katharine was determined to be independent. She planned her small rebellion and looked to a career that would somehow combine music and writing. She moved into a tiny apartment in Greenwich Village with her childhood friend Dolly Adriance, who was studying pottery. Happily, Dolly's father paid all their bills! Katharine studied piano, taught music at Christadora settlement house and found a job with Publisher's Weekly. The Roaring Twenties were yet to come, but the "fast 12th Street Set" as they called themselves, emerged — a group of dedicated, serious young college graduates who would be well known in time for their artistic and literary achievements. Katharine was exhilarated to be in the company of vibrant contemporaries, surrounded by art, music and stimulating conversation. As they cooked scrambled eggs over a gas jet, they pondered the fate of mankind and encouraged each other to create great things. The desire to be recognized as an artist burned inside Katharine. She decided "I was a female Hemingway and my ambition soared to such an extent I scarcely ate or slept as I typed up articles and short stories that sprang full grown into my head." Over the years she sold more than 250 stories, poems and articles, and published several songs. But hers was a divided life, for she could not decide whether to be a musician or a writer. She would say later: "I loved music too much to give it up and try writing, and loved writing too much to give it up for music. I divided my time between the two and thus never completely conquered either."

Swept up in the creative life of post-war New York, Katharine yearned to make her mark in the world and become financially independent. Her upbringing, however, predestined her to be a wife and mother. Just as she couldn't choose between music and writing, so she was ambivalent about combining marriage, motherhood and a profession. The time had not come for women to make a clear choice, because few men honestly believed in equal rights for both sexes. Her family assumed, of course, that a fling in New York was but a prelude to marriage and domesticity. But for Katharine, an intellectual with great creative talent, the situation was frustrating. And the problem was doubly difficult as she couldn't decide between her two demanding disciplines, music and writing. Another side of her, however, longed for the great romance that had been denied her mother, and the warmth and fulfilling joy of happy family life. For someone with a less idealistic nature, or perhaps greater creative talent and determination, the path would have been easier. But in 1921 she had not made a name for herself in the literary or musical worlds and had not, as yet, fallen in love. As it turned out, her life was about to change.

# Chapter Twelve
## Romance Yes, Domesticity No

Down the Bluff from Sunnycliffe lived Katharine's good friend Agnes Rogers, later to become an author and wife of social historian Frederick Lewis Allen, Editor of Harper's Magazine. Agnes' beau was Rudolph Stanley-Brown whose sister Ruth was a Vassar classmate of both Agnes' and Katharine's. In time Ruth would work as an editor for *The Dial* in New York before she married Herbert Feis, a brilliant and influential economist in the Roosevelt administration.

*Rudolph Stanley-Brown,*
*Captain, Artillery, 1917*

Rudolph, a graduate of Yale and Sheffield School of Engineering, had fallen in love with France when he studied architecture at the Beaux Arts in Paris before World War I. In 1917, he joined the Army and saw action on the Western Front as a Captain of artillery. Later he became aide to General Hines, and then to General John J. Pershing, commander-in-chief of the American Expeditionary Force in Europe. When the war ended in November, 1918, Rudolph was asked to stay on in Saumur to translate the manuals for American field guns into French. It was easier, the Army reasoned, to leave large pieces of artillery in France with instructions for their use, than to bring them back to America. Rudolph (who always wished he had been christened Richard) was named for his grandmother, Lucretia Rudolph, who had married his grandfather, James Abram Garfield, 20th President of the United States. And in 1917, he was writing letters from near the front lines in France to Agnes Rogers in Nantucket. She, in turn, tossed the pages to Katharine who read, not about the war, but with a growing fascination, about art and architecture.

In the last days of 1921, Ruth Stanley-Brown invited Katharine to spend the New Year's weekend at her family's house on Long Island. The big excitement was Rudolph's homecoming after five years in France. As the story goes, he burst into the house, spied a sprig of mistletoe hanging between the hall and dining room, was introduced to Katharine, dropped his suitcase, put his arms around her and kissed her. Saturday he took her to the Café Royale in New York for dinner, champagne, dancing, and non-stop conversation. When they got back to Long Island late that night, Katharine spilled a bottle of milk all over the kitchen floor. She was appalled and burst out crying but Rudy, as she always called him, laughed, cleaned it up, and kissed away her tears. Sunday morning dawned sunny and cold with a light coating of snow on the ground. The two went for a walk. Katharine's words: "We knew by then that we liked each other enough and understood each other too well for any mere proposal to be necessary. We stopped on a wide snow-covered playground and Rudy picked up a long stick and began drawing the outline of a house in the snow. 'There are only three basic floor plans,' he said, marking out each one. 'Which one shall I build for you when we're married?'"

The time was right for both of them. Katharine was 30 and Rudy was 34. In him, Katharine had found her ideal: a talented, creative, cultured man who wanted to care for her. He was a person of aesthetic sensibility who appreciated art and beauty. He was gentle yet strong. He had perspective on life and, best of all, he had a sense of humor. He was completely different from her duty-bound, sober-sided, religious relatives. Life hadn't dealt Rudy the blows it had the Henrys and Olivers. In Paris he learned to laugh and take life as it came. For Katharine, he was a dream of happiness come true. She already knew and liked his two sisters, and soon came to love his gentle, home-loving mother, Molly, the only daughter of President Garfield. Rudy responded to Katharine's love of the arts, her romantic temperament, and her facile mind. In fact, he found her perfect in every way.

They were married on June 6, 1922 at Grace Church, East Orange, New Jersey, as Katharine's parents had been. Rudy had a cadre of ushers — friends, Beaux Arts classmates, and Garfield cousins. Katrina Stephenson, Katharine's favorite young cousin, clad in apricot silk with a wide-brimmed brown picture hat, was her only attendant. The reception in the garden was festive with sheaves of beautiful flowers sent from Philadelphia by Mary's dear friend, David Williams. Champagne flowed and guests were given a sit-down "wedding breakfast." The placecards were decorated with French châteaux drawn and painted by Rudy. Then farewells, and the newlyweds were off for six weeks to Rudy's beloved France, and three weeks in England.

They traveled by train to Quebec City and then by steamer across the Atlantic. Their budget was Left Bank, but their happiness was Right Bank! They traveled by train and stopped in small towns to buy picnic lunches. After lunch, Rudy sketched or did watercolors of the town's best architectural features — churches, street scenes or châteaux — while Katharine wrote. Their illustrated articles appeared in architectural magazines during the 1920s and 1930s. The newlyweds visited museums, ate entrecôtes and pommes frites washed down with Nuits-St. Georges and came back speaking French like natives. In Cleveland, Rudy joined his Uncle Abram Garfield's architectural firm and Katharine sat down in their tiny, rented house to write 1,200 thank-you notes.

Socially, Cleveland was a far cry from Greenwich Village. If Rudy had had his way, they would have lived permanently in Paris. They both hated the social conventions and rigidity of life, but for eleven years they couldn't afford to leave. Katharine dreaded Sunday nights when they were expected to appear at Rudy's Uncle Abe and Aunt Ray Garfield's house in Bratenahl.

*Katharine Oliver on her wedding day—June 6, 1922*

Aunt Ray was small but domineering and it was a required ritual that Katharine play two pianos with her after dinner. Although she loved the music, she disliked playing on demand. Rudy, who could hardly refuse to spend Sunday evenings with his boss, didn't bother to be upset, but read his way happily through his uncle's vast collection of Civil War books.

Paradoxically, although they disliked life in Cleveland, Katharine and Rudy were at their creative best during these years. They collaborated on many articles and three books, all related to art, music and literature. In 1927, Harper & Brothers published their first book, *The Song Book of the American Spirit*, containing 30 songs that Katharine felt represented historic and patriotic music of national significance. She wrote out the harmonies that a young pianist could learn, and Rudy illustrated each page. She told a book reviewer that the idea came to her because she enjoyed singing French nursery songs to her four-year old son and thought that he should hear authentic American songs as well. The book sold well and Harper's asked them to write another for teenagers on the history of printing as part of its new City and Country Series. *The History of Printed Pictures* was published in 1928, and *The Young Architects* came out in 1931. In 1929, Rudolph illustrated another book in the series, *The Young Decorators*, written by Nancy McClellan.

But Cleveland stifled them. They were both in their 30's, full of creative energy and ambition, but not wealthy enough to keep up with their friends. Architects didn't earn a living on the same scale as doctors, lawyers or businessmen, and when the stock marked crashed in 1929, people who had hoped to build large, private houses changed their plans. In a letter to Katharine during this period, Rudy noted with pleasure that he had a job remodeling a barn. Yet, by all standards, the young couple lived comfortably with a cook, a laundress, and as soon as they had a child, a daytime nurse.

Being able to spend summers at Nantucket was a godsend in many ways, particularly for Katharine. She went to pieces in the summer heat, and in 1923, when she was pregnant with her first child, she was plagued with severe morning sickness and fatigue for months. Rudy, always concerned for her welfare, urged her to stay on the Island as long as possible. Also, Katharine wanted to be with her mother whom she missed. Less altruistically, with Katharine and later with the children in Nantucket, the financial burden was eased for Rudy who could let the cook and maid go and take care of himself. He was an excellent cook and had lots of friends who entertained him.

But aside from other reasons, Katharine loved Nantucket as much as any place she had been. It was the one stable home that she had known all her life. In later years she wondered if she had chosen wisely to be away from her husband every summer for three or four months, but at the time it seemed the right thing to do. She missed Rudy, yearned for his August arrival and made plans for the lovely things they would do together. Their letters are intimate and loving, thoughtful and empathetic. Early in their marriage they had agreed to be completely honest with each other in all things, so she spared him nothing of her thoughts and activities, as well as the difficulties at Sunnycliffe. Katharine hated dissonance, and worried herself to the point of illness over family relationships, the management of servants, and her own psyche. Rudy, with his calm yet lighthearted perspective on life, could keep her balanced. He never judged or criticized her actions, but reassured her with unequivocal love and admiration. In any crisis that occurred at Sunnycliffe, he took her side and did what he could to smooth over the situation. His response was often "Think nothing of it." But, without Rudy, she was often distraught.

Four months before my brother Teddy was born in 1923, Katharine felt she would be losing her freedom for a long time to come, and she had no particular affinity for the baby she was carrying. Yet, she knew that Nantucket was the healthiest place for her to be. In one violent outburst she wrote to Rudy: "It is so dull. I don't see a soul — I haven't seen a *man* to speak of in two weeks and you know I *much* prefer men to women. No one really notices you when you're married — still less when you're having babies and I feel hopelessly unpopular. Your two letters just came and, of course, I'm glad you're so gay and going on picnics and dances and playing tennis — but tonight I feel awfully rebellious and as if I'd just plain die if I couldn't have a little fun."

If Cleveland was boring, in its own way Nantucket was, too. Katharine loved her husband but craved the attention of other men and hated pregnancy. How sad to be caught between a Victorian upbringing and the emerging feeling on the part of women that they should have equal rights and opportunities. Marriage with Rudy was wonderful and satisfying, but motherhood loomed as a threat to their relationship and to her writing career. Had she been a distinguished author or musician, she might have chosen differently. Rudy's youngest sister Peggy gave up any thoughts of marriage to become a surgeon in New York, and was perfectly happy with her decision. Her career was a rewarding one and she was widely respected in her field.

When she retired from surgery in her late fifties, she did marry and then with the joy and excitement of a 22-year-old!

In spite of the letters she wrote, it's apparent that Katharine and her friends at least seemed to have had fun on Nantucket during the 1920s. They played badminton, quoits (a close cousin to horseshoes) and croquet on the coarse grass lawns, golfed at the new Sankaty Golf Club or played tennis at the Casino. They met on the beach, lay on the warm sand talking about books, music, theater and love, and ate raw clams for lunch. When their husbands came for vacations, they planned clam bakes, beach picnics and dinners to fill every moment. There were concerts at the Casino, and weekend dances at the Yacht Club and the Golf Club. The cocktail party didn't yet exist as an institution, but somehow, in spite of Prohibition, Katharine always had a bottle of whiskey for entertaining. There were cooks, waitresses and nurses in most households to relieve mothers of the mechanical aspects of domestic care. Indeed, despite Katharine's complaints, these young women could be said to have lead charmed lives!

When Rudy came to Sconset, however, he and Katharine preferred to be alone on a deserted beach or on the Moors. There wasn't enough time to be together on his all too short vacations. Rudy and the sun weren't compatible, so except for an occasional snapshot of him in a bathing suit, he is always pictured at the beach in a suit and hat.

Katharine said herself that she was a reluctant mother, but she loved Rudy enough to go through the discomforts of pregnancy twice. Although she adored Teddy, her first born and a

*Rudolph Stanley-Brown with his two sisters—Ruth S-B. Feis and Peggy—Kew Gardens, 1934*

son, Katharine longed for some time of her own. An author and intellect, she was bored with formula, bottles, dirty diapers, and what she considered the menial and mechanical tasks of baby-rearing. Mary agreed, and, in the fashion of the day, hired a baby nurse each summer. Although she supervised the daily routine for Teddy, Katharine took direct care of him only when the nurse had her Thursday and half Sundays off. What distressed Katharine most, she reported, were the natural activities of babies — crying, wetting, and waking up at night. In later years, she said she had followed the advice of a popular baby expert of the day, a Dr. Watson, who advocated not picking up, cuddling and comforting an unhappy baby. Attention should be paid to their needs on a strict schedule, he advised, and in time the baby would learn to conform. No-nonsense toilet-training started early and babies less than a year old, were left on their potties for hours until they "performed." When they didn't adhere to Dr. Watson's time table, they were considered uncooperative and even naughty.

Teddy was almost five years old when I was born in 1928. Katharine's letters to Rudy during my infancy reveal a continuing dislike of the mechanics of child care and an annoyance with the interruptions in her life that infants caused. She loved us when we met her adult behavior standards, but had no patience with us when, in her view, we misbehaved. For someone who responded to so much of life intellectually, it's puzzling that she didn't understand early childhood, and take an interest in *why* we acted as we did. Punishment, doled out on numerous occasions, never fitted the crime. She spanked us, sent us to bed early without supper, and on occasion, shut Teddy in a closet. Or she would not let us have sugar on our cereal! In one letter to Rudy she wrote: "the baby (that was me) ate a whole box of candy and had to be disciplined."

Just before I was born, Katharine and Rudy sent four-year old Teddy off to spend a month with his Stanley-Brown grandparents, and then three months with Mary. Shut off from an exciting family event, he must have felt very unloved. He was adored by his grandparents, but it was a hard time for a little boy to be away from his family.

For many years the solution to Katharine's dislike of babyhood was to have fulltime help and to separate her children. In the few summers when Teddy and I were at Sunnycliffe together, he was sent off to play with other little boys his own age. Teddy, nearly five years old than I am, was alternately jealous, a bully, or a tease. As a little boy he was, according to Katharine, lazy, untidy, uncooperative and thoughtless. Her letters to Rudy are litanies of complaint. "Teddy refuses to . . .", "Teddy was naughty again . . .", and sometimes "Teddy seems slightly improved." Although I didn't behave the way Katharine wanted me to — I threw temper tantrums when I didn't get my way and whined — it was different. After all, I was the baby! Teddy would hardly know that he was jealous, and used what defenses he had to tease me or to make me cry. I adored my big brother and tried to be included when he played with his friends. When he refused to take me with him, I shrieked with anger and frustration.

As a last measure, when Katharine could no longer bear our bickering and screaming, she sent one or the other of us to spend part of each summer with the Stanley-Brown grandparents in Kew Gardens. I remember having a marvelous time with them. There were trips to the beach, into New York for shopping at Altman's, and lunch at Schrafft's on Fifth Avenue. Gramps was an enthusiastic gardener and I loved helping him and feeding the huge goldfish in the garden pool. He grew what I consider to be old-fashioned flowers. Coreopsis, calendula, hollyhocks, ranunculus and linaria are some of the marvelous names I remember. The only thing I disliked about visiting Gramps was that he listened to Gabriel Heatter deliver the news every night on the radio at 6 p.m., just at the time I wanted to hear the adventures of Jack Armstrong, the All American Boy, and to learn the benefits of Ovaltine and Borden's Ice Cream from the commercials. With only one classic dark brown, gothic-arched, Philco radio set, Gramps won and I lost.

Gran was a true homemaker. She taught me to knit, make cookies, and preserve watermelon pickle. She had a Kitchen Aid mixer and I marveled at how quickly she could make a fluffy yellow cake or frosting. But both Teddy and I, at least subconsciously, resented being shunted back and forth, and missed our parents, our friends, and Nantucket immensely. For us, the Island became the symbol of all that was fun and pleasant, of family happiness and freedom.

*"Gran"—Mary Garfiield Stanley-Brown*

Katharine's impatience with her children may be explained in part by her health. Beginning in 1930 she suffered from daily headaches, so severe that she spent much of the day in bed. Doctors in New Jersey, New York and Ohio failed to find a cause, either physical or psychological. Even the famous brain surgeon, Harvey Cushing, who was also consulted, was stumped. The pain was worse when she had menstrual periods, but diagnosis seemed impossible. Naturally, rest and quiet were difficult to find with the demands of a boisterous young family and the Sunnycliffe household. Mary made every effort to help Katharine by ordering her breakfasts in bed, nurses for the children, and by easing the daily schedule so that she could go off by herself to write or just lie on the beach. But constant pain is debilitating, and it is a credit to Katharine's spirit that she remained at least fairly cheerful and creatively productive during this difficult period.

# Chapter Thirteen
## Behind the Scenes

What would Sunnycliffe have been like without servants? Well, obviously, it would have been very different existence. Mary did beautiful embroidery and sang, and Katharine could make orange marmalade and penuche fudge. Norris washed dishes and in later life learned how to launder his own drip-dry shirt. However, it was only because the house was full of skilled and devoted helpers that the Olivers, the Henrys and the Stanley-Browns were able to enjoy life as they did between 1889 and 1940.

The economic climate of those years made it possible to hire household workers for a nominal wage. Immigrants and minorities from the New York area — and many who worked for Mary in the summer were black or Hispanic — were only too glad to have a steady job. They knew how to work long hours and, for the most part, were honest, uncomplaining and flexible. And employment at a pleasant summer resort meant escaping the discomforts and often the diseases of hot and dirty cities.

Although Mary was a kind employer, she had uncommonly high standards as well as her own idiosyncrasies and anyone who worked for her had to be ready for the unexpected. "There'll be ten for lunch today," she would say with a smile at 9 a.m. Or the weather would turn and plans for a picnic would be cancelled. "We'll all be here for dinner tonight, so you'll have to change your day off." If the cook or maids wanted to attend church, they had to walk a mile each way to the Sconset Chapel which held Episcopal services and Catholic Mass as well as a Baptist service every Sunday evening. Trips into Nantucket town were infrequent, especially for the "help."

Life at Sunnycliffe, too, was only slightly less formal than in Philadelphia. In the 1890's, Mary brought her butler, Sylvanus Johnson, up for the summer, as well as a cook and a maid. Any

*Sylvanus Johnson*

other help that was needed came from the Island. The servants who lived in, occupied two tiny attic rooms, often hot and stuffy in mid-summer. There was one bathroom on the second floor and an outhouse off the kitchen. Only when Sunnycliffe got running water in 1900 was a second bath built for servants' use.

In Sconset Mary's relationship with her help was difficult. The size of the house and its layout made privacy impossible. Neither family nor servants could get away from each other. There was a small porch off the kitchen where the cook and maids could relax between chores, but it was in clear view of the back road, and Mary would often hear from a friend: "Why, I saw your cook sitting on the porch with her feet up — and at four in the afternoon!"

In 1923, the cook, Helen, developed such bad foot trouble that everyone feared she might not be able to work. Katharine, pregnant and having trays in bed, wrote Rudy: "That *would* be a calamity up here." Helen was concerned about other feet as well, those of the noisy little field mice who ran between the walls of most Sconset houses. Thomas Clifton, the handyman for many years, opened up the upstairs wall and baited mouse traps with cheese. Of course, the mice were unthwarted and continued to build their nests either in the linen closet or among the wool blankets. Fourteen years later there were still complaints. That summer, Mary, the cook from Orange, objected that "rats got in the bureau and left their young."

Rosa came in 1926 to cook for 20 dollars a week. She was described as "an excellent servant who never complains and is kind and efficient." She must have been a saint, for the household changed constantly. Mary, Katharine and then three-year old Teddy, a baby nurse and maid were present all summer. Jay and Norris came and went. Lewie and Margaret made two, week-long visits. Seven Carters, five Stephensons and, without warning, the Connett family from England, appeared. The demands on the cook were enormous and unending. Sometimes, no one took a day off and Rosa was lucky if she had an hour to herself in the afternoon.

By 1929, life was complex enough to exhaust everyone. Lewie, in one of his impetuous but generous gestures, had decided to build Mary her own bathroom. This meant taking half the space of the room next to Mary's, changing walls and rearranging plumbing. Seven workmen were busy most of June and July, hammering and pounding away all day. The noise was particularly upsetting to Katharine who suffered from what she described as mysterious "knocking headaches" and spent most mornings in bed. Teddy was six and I was one plus, in the care of Louise Lopez-Cardoza. She was an excellent baby nurse but, as was the case with many "nannies," she held herself above general domestic service and drew the line at having anything to do with the preparation and delivery of our food. Thus the maid was expected to carry trays, set tables, clean up, do laundry and and sweep and dust the house. Understandably, she complained of the work load. By August, the household staff had rebelled. The cook refused to get the children's trays ready and grumbled that Louise never washed up the dishes. Each had a grievance when asked to step beyond the perceived limits of her job. But Katharine, who loathed conflict, somehow managed skillfully to molify all three and cajole them into staying for the summer.

In 1930, the cook and Florence the waitress arrived on July third and the next day Katharine wrote Rudy that "the new maids are perfectly dumb — the waitress has never waited before and yet had the nerve to come, and the cook cooks badly, but Mother is tackling them fiercely and they may learn." Mary spent the early weeks of each summer instructing new help, and in this case, Florence had to learn the difference between a knife and a teaspoon and where to place them on the table. Five days of instruction may have been useful, but on July eight life came to a standstill. The cook burned her hand too badly to work in the kitchen and Loretta, the baby nurse for that summer, had sprained her ankle. Neither Mary nor Katharine was prepared to take over, so everyone just waited and went to restaurants for meals!

In only two days, Loretta was walking, but in considerable pain. The cook was back at the stove, although she couldn't wash dishes. Her arm ached and the burns, still bandaged and salved, had yet to heal. Mary and Katharine made sure the servants had prompt medical attention, but it was not done in those days to give them time off to recover. Without health insurance, workmen's compensation, or an advocate for their rights, servants everywhere simply played through. So gamely in fact, that by mid-July Loretta said that she could cope with both children if Katharine needed to get away and rest. And Florence, the maid, was at least relieved of one chore. Mary sent all the laundry back to East Orange.

Marie replaced Loretta as a baby nurse in 1931, although I don't think she lasted very long. Then age four, I offered to trim

*Marie—Summer baby nurse in 1930 with Katharine O. Stanley-Brown*

her toenails and by mistake cut off the top of her third toe! Florence stayed for five summers and learned to wait, to clean and even to produce acceptable meals when the cook was out. She coped with the volatile household, Katharine's continuing headaches, noisy children and Mary's moods. Only once, in 1934, did she announce that she had a "nervous breakdown" from working in the house, but gamely declared she would try to stick it out.

By the summer of 1931, Mary's diabetes was under control, as much as it could be in those days. Mary usually accepted man's fate as God's will, but as the disease tightened its grip she became resentful and imperious. And in the years that followed, as she lost her eyesight, the prospect of facing a life of darkness terrified her. She refused to be left alone, sought to be involved in what the household did and demanded Katharine's time. The burden of Mary's comfort and happiness fell on Katharine's shoulders during the summer as she also coped with two children, her sometimes difficult brother Norris, and a husband too far away to keep her balanced emotionally. And, of course, her own health was far from good.

Rudolph Stanley-Brown, 1932

Quite suddenly, a year later, in 1932, Rudy developed diabetes as well. "I know," his mother said, "that it was because he had such bad food during the war." He, too, learned about the disease at the Joslin Clinic, but unlike Mary, he refused to let it take over his life. He had such an optimistic attitude and sense of perspective that few people knew he was sick. That year also he and Katharine contemplated moving to Nantucket year-round where life would be simpler. He would design houses, produce etchings and paint, and she would write. Teddy and I would go to local schools. But before that decision was really made Rudy received a call from Washington.

Among his many programs for the country, President Franklin D. Roosevelt, then newly-elected, proposed to improve the city of Washington's "Federal Character". In addition, he proposed a plan to design public buildings such as post offices, schools and court houses around the country that would showcase an area's history, local architectural style and indigenous materials. He asked Rudy to join a group of distinguished young American architects to implement his proposal. Despite a firm family association with the Republican Party, Roosevelt's progressive ideas for the troubled nation appealed to them both. It was a great honor and it meant fascinating new challenges in architecture in an era when building in the private sector had been severely curtailed by the Depression. Both Rudy and Katharine leapt at the chance to leave Cleveland and to start a new life in Washington, working for ideals they believed in. Thus began an exciting career for Rudy, both in designing public buildings and in his own architectural career. President Roosevelt was an amateur architect himself with a strong sense of design and history, so it's not surprising that one of Rudy's most important jobs was working directly with the President to design post offices for the towns of Hyde Park, Rhinebeck and Wappinger's Falls, all close to the Roosevelt's own home in Hyde Park. All three are standing today and combine elements of old Dutch architecture which prevailed in towns along the Hudson River. All three are built of fieldstone, a widely-used building material of the area.

The nation's capital is unbearably hot and humid in the summer, and was even more difficult for Katharine to endure than Cleveland. Rudy, whose circulation was poor as a result of diabetes, rather enjoyed the hot weather, but he urged Katharine to spend summers at Nantucket. With Mary sick, she also felt a duty to be there. Her mother was almost blind by the summer of 1935 and Lewie insisted that his sister have two maids whose wages he paid. A combination trained nurse, secretary and companion, Miss Katharine Ulmar spent the summer, and a young girl, Mary Skeats, lived at Sunnycliffe for a month. She read to Mary, did some sewing and mending, and shared breakfast with me on the front porch. Again, Lewie was sensitive to his sister's needs and gave her, as he described it, a "very fine General Electric refrigerator." Not only did it make life easier in the kitchen, but it solved the problem of keeping Mary's insulin properly chilled. Although she couldn't see, Mary's assessment of the household help that summer was: "the cook is very neat and kindly . . . both [servants] are very attentive to me." However, Katharine saw things differently. "The cook is a very poor one," she wrote Rudy, "so it is lucky I am on a diet. They are very poor servants, both cross, always arguing."

In 1936, Mary engaged a Baptist minister and his wife to run the kitchen for the summer. He had one request, that they be allowed to leave Sunday night supper on the stove so that he could preach at the Sconset Chapel. Mary agreed and outlined her summer routine carefully, stressing, as she had always, the importance of homemade food.

The summer started well enough. One Sunday night, however, the minister and his wife hurried off to the Chapel, leaving Campbell's tomato soup warming on the stove. We all sat down

to supper enjoying the soup course until I said, with the innocence of my eight years, that it was delicious — for canned
soup. My grandmother was outraged. "How dare they!" she
exploded. "I told them specifically that I required homemade
food and they have purposely disobeyed my orders. They will
have to go." Back came the minister and his wife from their
evening of spiritual uplifting. The next morning Mary, still
seething and capricious as always, fired them on the spot.
Incredible as it sounds there was no talking it over, no second
chance, just out the door. As with many other problems at
Sunnycliffe, if there was a way to make an minor incident into a
major catastrophe, someone surely did.

From 1936 on, Katharine took charge of Sunnycliffe, but not
without resentment. She still suffered from severe headaches,
but was expected to handle everything. She ordered the meals,
marketed, chauffeured the family around, managed the nurses,
comforted her mother, and then tried to find time to write and
to see her friends. Mary was increasingly difficult and demanding of those who cared for her. She found fault with nurses and
fired them, leaving Katharine and Norris to find new ones.
Since Mary couldn't see, she insisted on being told about everything and included in all family activities. Her nurses were
exhausted answering questions and if Katharine looked in to
see her mother, the nurse on duty fled for a few moments of
relief from Mary's incessant demands.

Life was easier in 1937 because Mary Washington, the kind
and devoted black cook from Orange, came for the summer. She
was cheerful, and the meals she prepared were delicious, so her
appearance had a bolstering effect on the household. Mary
Washington had worked in a bakery for $48 a week (twice what
Mary Oliver paid her) and her bread, rolls, doughnuts and pies
were heavenly creations. My brother recalls that when she
made blueberry pie at Sunnycliffe, she always made an extra
one just for him. Poor Mary, however, had painful corns on her
toes and so went around barefoot most of that summer. I must
have been impressed with this because I wrote my mother a
postcard (she was in Washington later than usual that year) and
drew a picture of Mary, barefoot. It was lucky for Mary
Washington that Mary Oliver could not see for she would never
have allowed such behavior.

The summer of 1938 was unusually hot, even for
Nantucket. Mosquitoes were a constant annoyance and the
maids complained of the work load. Rudy wrote Katharine:
"They are the kind who would complain if they were in

Heaven." Trying to help, he wrote to Mary's day nurse, Ruth MacCracken, urging her to put fewer demands on Katharine. Nurse MacCracken replied: "Everything seems to be running smoothly. Mrs. Stanley-Brown has left nothing undone for the comfort and well-being of all of us." Although her first duty was to her patient, she assured him she would do what she could to give Katharine time to rest. "Mrs. Oliver and I do seem to get along very well indeed," she went on, "because I try to put myself in her place should the conditions be reversed." In spite of her sympathetic tone, Nurse MacCracken could not do much to help lighten Katharine's load. However much she complained, in the fashion of her family Katharine put "duty before pleasure" because, of course, what else could she do? Here, for instance, is her day on August 4, 1938, a she described it in a letter to Rudy:

8:30 a.m. - Ordered meals by telephone
    Wire from Wambaughs who arrive 2:00 p.m. boat
    Siki appeared - John L.'s eye closed, could I take him to doctor?
9:00 a.m. - Mrs. Clark called. Wambaughs could stay with her.
9:30 a.m. - Mrs. Clark reneged. Try for another room.
11:00 a.m. - Took children and nurse swimming.
1:10 p.m. - Lunch late. Mother, nurse, two children and me fed and in car by 1:30.
2:15 p.m. - Got to dock as boat pulled in. Met Wambaughs, got last two seats on bus and told them where to go. Teddy to algebra tutor's.
    Mother to chiropodist to cut out two ingrown toenails.
    Took front porch cushions to be recovered. Drugstore, bank.
    To Dr. Menges to have sand washed out of my ear.
4:00 p.m. - Back for Mother and Teddy.
    To Sconset, stop for mail.
    Home to find telegram from D (Dolly Caracciolo). She'll be on midnight boat and please get her car over to boat.
4:30 p.m. - Wambaughs appeared for swim.
    John G. to see Teddy.
    Mademoiselle and three Laylins came to call.
    Tea, then took all to beach.
6:00 p.m. - Gave them all highballs.
    Teddy appeared with message Mrs. Zerbe wanted me to dinner. Told him to say no, he forgot until half way through dinner.
    Teddy telephoned Mrs. Zerbe with apology.
    Trying dinner - night nurse complained of heat, mosquitoes and said fish (delicious little butter fish) was all bones.

8:00 p.m. - Dressed Kay up and took her to dance. Sat and
watched.
9:30 p.m. - Kay and I home. Teddy went to older dance.

On less hectic days Mary loved to sit on the front porch and
chat with whoever walked up the Bluff to see her. She always
dressed in white — a long high-necked white dress, white
stockings and shoes, and straw hat. There she would greet her
friends and catch up on the social life of Sconset. She loved
being read to, particularly by Katharine, whose skill as a writer
gave special drama to a book. And there were always long, loving letters to her family, to Rudy in Washington, to Teddy or to
me if we were off Island, dictated to a nurse or secretary. Mary
enjoyed dictating, so her letters were chatty and informal.

On August 12, Mary Oliver apparently suffered a stroke.
She was very weak, could hardly walk, sobbed and clung to
Nurse MacCracken. Norris, on the Island for his vacation, took
a hand in ordering the nurses about and stirred things up so
much, according to Katharine, that the exasperated night nurse
was rude. She was fired and sent back to Newark, but a
Nantucket nurse was found right away who proved to be calm
and efficient.

Five days later, Katharine thought her mother had a strange
look and wouldn't pull through. Her leg was paralyzed and by
the next day she was semi-conscious and speechless. She was
taken to the Nantucket Cottage Hospital when she developed a
fever and couldn't swallow. After ten days, however, she rallied
and Norris exclaimed: "she's been spared for us!" Katharine,
less optimistic, wrote Rudy that it would be a blessing if Mary
died; she was miserable. Once again, everything fell on
Katharine's shoulders. On Labor Day, Norris, Jay and Lewie
went back to New York, leaving her to manage the hospital, to
deal with the servants, and to close Sunnycliffe. The men handled all the bills, but still Katharine resented the role she was
asked to play. As she wrote to Rudy on August 25: "I do not
intend to return here next year and I do not intend to own this
house hereafter jointly with Norris."

Mary died on October 12, 1938 in East Orange and
Sunnycliffe was left to Norris and Katharine. Whatever she said
to the contrary, the two of them shared summers there for the
next 34 years with affection and good will. Curiously that fall,
Katharine's headaches stopped altogether after she had a hys-
terectomy. My brother, a surgeon, believes that the headaches
were caused by tension, stress and untreated high blood pres-

sure. Considering what life was like in Sunnycliffe, he may be right!

Mary Washington ruled the Sunnycliffe kitchen for several more years, but World War II brought about the end of domestic service as it had been known. There were still people on the Island to do heavy work. Chris Psaradelis clipped the privet hedges and cut back the wild rose. George Rogers tended the aging plumbing when he wasn't teaching Sconset teenagers the fine art of surf casting. And John Santos was a combination carpenter, handy man and caretaker who put the house to bed in the fall and opened it in June. Like many Sconseters, he was descended from whaling men who had made their way to Nantucket from the Cape Verde Islands. Three hundred and eighty-five miles off Africa's west coast, the Islands were settled by the Portuguese in 1465. During the 1850's, Nantucket whalers were having trouble enlisting crews. Captain Gonzalves, en route to southern whaling grounds, stopped at the Cape Verdean island of Brava. In the mid-19th century, drought and famine had severely depressed the economy of Brava and young men flocked to sign on as crew on U.S. whalers. Eventually, as the whaling industry died out, the Cape Verdeans migrated to Nantucket and New Bedford where they settled down and found other occupations.

Of all the devoted servants who worked for the Henrys and the Olivers, Chappell Brown was the one who made the family his own. Brown, as everyone called him, was born into a large black farming family at Amelia Court House, Virginia. He had had one other job — six months as an orderly in a Richmond hospital — when he came to work for Catherine Henry as a butler at 26 Washington Street, East Orange. There he stayed for 42 years. He married, had three children and lived in nearby Orange, but he was at the Henrys' house every morning at 7:30 a.m. and often stayed until 9:30 or 10 at night. He learned when to speak and when to remain silent, to clean, wax floors, polish brass, silver and leather, and to wait on the table. After Mary Oliver died he even learned to cook.

Lewie, Jay and Norris gave him clothing, showed him how to invest his money, and presented his children bicycles, thick coats and whatever else they needed at Christmas. Brown loved children and my mother remembered that when she came to East Orange to live at the age of ten, he became her special friend. She had loved her mother's butler, Sylvanus Johnson in Philadelphia, too. The question of color was never an issue. These two gentle and kind men gave her the affection and attention she needed when she was a lonely and bewildered little girl.

When Norris died in 1962, Katharine walked to the graveside services with her arm on Brown's to the surprise of relatives who thought she would walk with her son. A perceptive cousin remarked that it wasn't at all strange. "Did you ever think," she said, "of all they have been through together and that Katharine may be more fond of Brown than she is of any of the family?" I think Katharine would have said that Brown was her last link with the past.

After the East Orange house was emptied and sold, Brown spent two winters with Katharine in Washington and often told her fascinating stories about the family as her served her dinner. As she reported, he might start back to the kitchen with a plate, turn and say: "Did you ever happen to hear why your Aunt Louise moved to Boston to live?", telling her something she had never known before. Sadly, chronic asthma made working too difficult as Brown got older and for his last years he moved back to New Jersey to live with one of his married daughters.

Like many families of their ilk, the Henrys and Olivers took for granted that they would be cared for by their "faithful retainers". How different their lives would have been without them! World War II altered the structure of society forever, and for those born after 1945, the life I've described in Sconset must seem extraordinary and unreal. I hardly remember the cooks, maids, and baby nurses who came and went during my childhood, and the thought of managing such a household today seems both antiquated and exhausting.

# *Chapter Fourteen*
# *Neighbors*

When Sunnycliffe was built in 1887, it was one of the few summer cottages on Sconset's North Bluff. Vegetation in the area was sparse — scrub pine and stunted oak, elderberry and rosa rugosa. And there were no trees to shield the houses from the east wind that blew across the flat land.

Sea gulls and terns soared and dove with their lonely cry, and in the early morning, song birds called to each other, but for the most part, the only sound was the constant rush of wind. When it blew from the south, you could hear the surf, the long rollers breaking on the beach. At night, crickets chirped and hummed, and when the fog crept in, the horn at Sankaty Light moaned its warning to mariners offshore.

House lots were separated from each other by simple post and rail fences and a dirt path along the Bluff gave the public a pleasant walk from the Village to Sankaty Light. The poet Bliss Carman captured the spirit of Sconset's Bluff when he wrote in 1908:

*"The Path to Sankoty"—*
*Sunnycliffe circa 1900*

## The Path to Sankoty

### 1
It winds along the headland
Above the open sea —
The lonely moorland footpath
That leads to Sankoty.

### 2
The crooning sea spreads
  sailless
 And gray to the world's rim
Where hang the reeking fog-
  banks
Primordial and dim.

### 3
There fret the ceaseless
  currents,
And the eternal tide
Chafes over hidden shallows
Where the white horses ride.

### 4
The wistful, fragrant moor
  lands
Whose smile bids panic cease,
Lie treeless and cloud-shad-
  owed
In grave and lonely peace.

### 5
Across their flowing bosom
From the far end of day
Blow clean the great soft
  moor-winds
All sweet with rose and bay

### 6
A world as large and simple
As first emerged for man,
Cleared for the human drama,
Before the play began.

### 7
O well the soul must treasure
The calm that sets it free —
The vast and tender skyline,
The sea-turn's wizardry,

### 8
Solace of swaying grasses,
The friendship of sweet fern —
And in the world's confusion
Remembering, must yearn.

### 9
To tread the moorland footpath
That leads to Sankoty,
Hearing the field-larks shrilling
Beside the sailless sea.

Rosa rugosa, bayberry, elderberry, blackberry and coarse beach grass all tumbled down the bank to the beach, often over-running the sand. Poison ivy flourished, spreading its shiny reddish green leaves between other grasses.

Mary spent many summers taming the landscape. She planted Scotch broom that exploded in a blaze of yellow each summer, encouraged by the sandy soils. Fuschia rosa rugosa flowers in June gave way to orange-red rose hips that made delicious jelly or, for us children, great ammunition to pelt each other. Every summer Mary added sturdy plants. She trained clematis and trumpet vines on trellises, planted hydrangeas by the front steps, and kept a cutting garden of annuals on the sheltered, south side of the kitchen. She, and Katharine after her, loved flowers, and there was always a vase of fresh blossoms in the guest room to greet a visitor. An arrangement of bay leaves with tiny gray berries sat on the dining room table and gave off a distinct, almost medicinal aroma. Even now, the smell of bayberry means Nantucket to me.

*Mary Oliver's clematis at Sunnycliffe*

All the Sconset houses were built of white cedar shingles which turned silver with time. Their trim was dark green or white. Occasionally, a maverick house flaunted yellow or light blue shutters with cutouts of whales or flowers. None of the fancy brick or white clapboard found in Nantucket for Sconseters! Ours were summer cottages, necessarily simple and uniform. Some in the village were fancier, such as the large white house with pillars where I went for summer camp and which later belonged to Roy Larsen, the founding genius behind *Time, Life* and *Fortune*. His house was topped with a splendid widow's walk.

On the south side of Sunnycliffe stood a large three-story summer cottage, one of two built by State Senator Spooner in the 1880's, and put up for sale shortly afterwards. It was bought in 1902 by a popular and beautiful actress from Scranton, Pennsylvania named Bertha Galland. Miss Galland made a name for herself as a star of Broadway's light musicals to the horror of her staid father who disowned her. Bertha's mother, Anna, took her daughter's side and the two of them spent many happy years in Berthanna along with their chauffeur Emil, and Bertha's manager, John J. Donnelly.

Mary Oliver disapproved of her neighbor's theatrical life. "You must never go next door," she warned young Katharine, "because a wicked lady lives there." In spite of the snub, Bertha and Anna spent 30 years in the house until 1932 when they were both tragically killed in an automobile accident. Berthanna was left to Emil and in 1933, grief-stricken John Donnelly, my mother wrote, could be seen in a rocking chair on the front porch, weeping and looking out to sea. Katharine's friends from Washington, John and Dorothy Laylin, rented Berthanna for the next few summers. After that the house was vacant until 1939 when Selden Dickinson, a lawyer from Grosse Point, Michigan, learned that it was to be sold at auction for back taxes. He bid $1,500 and won! He and his family moved in, renamed the

General and Mrs. Malvern
Hill Barnum

house Thickly Settled, and have been there ever since. So much did they love the old house that when it burned to the ground in the early 1980's, they built an almost exact replica, only slightly modernized. And, after some effort, Jerry Dickinson (my contemporary and friend) who owned the house after buying his two sisters out, found a golden oak player-piano to take the place of the much-used and much-beloved one destroyed in the fire.

On the other side of Sunnycliffe, in the 1920's, Colonel and Mrs. Mackie built a charming shingled cottage with many modern appointments, among them central heating, which made their long stays comfortable. Mrs. Mackie had a grand piano and during the 1920's and 1930's she begged Katharine, who hated to be asked to perfom, to come over and entertain her guests. But Mrs. Mackie and Mary Oliver were dear friends, and Katharine could not refuse.

Gradually, more summer cottages appeared and Mary, who was both sociable and vigorous in her early years, walked up or down the Bluff daily, stopping often to visit and chat. Our neighbors did the same and this was, in fact, a regular form of social interaction. Among Mary's good friends were, to the south, Elsie Brush, whose daughter Natalie was a friend of Katharine's and later an author and playwright. Further down lived General and Mrs. Malvern Hill Barnum (he was named for a Civil War battle) and Mary Turlay Robinson who illustrated childrens' books. To the north, beyond the Mackies, was Miss Wilmerding in Flagship, now owned by Marjorie Benchley, widow of writer Nat Benchley whose father was the Hollywood actor, writer and humorist Robert Benchley. Both Marjorie and Nat's sons are well-known authors themselves. Peter's novels, *Jaws*, *Jaws 2*, and *The Deep*, have been made into films and have thrilled movie audiences, and Nat's children's books are delightful.

Next to Flagship was Mayflower, a glowering gray shingle cottage with a deep overhanging roof, owned by Anne Wilson. When I was a child stopping to visit her with my Uncle Norris, Miss Wilson scared me because she stuttered. Next to her's was a very large house, much grander than the other cottages, that belonged to the Morris sisters who, Teddy recalls, had one of Sconset's first motor cars as well as a liveried chauffeur. The house was of yellow clapboard with wide porches wrapped around the first floor and large picture windows facing the ocean. It was later owned by the Eugene Cashmans from Wilmington, Delaware, who needed space for a large family. In time, the Cashmans built a tennis court across the back road from their house, the only private court, as I recall, in the Village. The house next to the Morrises belonged to two members of the faculty at Wellesley College, the Mlles. Rueche and Heubener, who tutored Teddy in French. Next to them was Lewie's golfing pal, Stanley Swift.

For years Lewie owned a piece of land in the gully next to Mr. Swift. It would have been a beautiful house site, but he never built on it, preferring his Shimmo house with its warm, still water and magnificent view of Nantucket harbor. But Lewie loved Sconset and I think always hoped that he would live there one day in a tiny house on the Bluff. Continuing on up to Sankaty Light, were Teddy's friends the Watrouses. Warren Watrous and Teddy played together a lot, and I remember what I considered to be their greatest achievement, an underground miniature golf course. The amazing thing was that Warren's parents allowed the boys to dig up their entire front lawn! From Teddy's many visits to Warren's, we learned, however inaccurately, that the Watrouses ate interesting food that usually included seaweed — perhaps it was kelp — and put whipped cream on everything!

After Mrs. Mackie died, the John Scotts from Pittsburgh rented the house next door. Lucky for me, their daughter Marcia was just my age and we became good friends. During the late 1930's there were lots of families with children living on the Bluff. The Dickinsons next door had three; Jerry, my age, Mary, Teddy's age, and Liz, a bit older. Next to them were the Wicksers with two boys and a red-haired daughter Teddy's age. Teddy's friend Bill Glazier lived nearer the Village, and on the corner of Butterfly Lane in a bright blue house with yellow shutters were the Grouts, with two daughters who played beautiful tennis, and a son John who liked to fish with Teddy at Gibbs Pond. Across from the Glaziers was my friend Marcia Cunningham, whose father Bill was a sports writer and columnist for *The Boston Herald*.

Ginny Vaughan, dark-haired and glamorous, blonde and boisterous Babs Widdoes, and the three handsome Frame boys all lived on the north side of the Village. There were others: Bob Blanchard, Ed Kern, the two Block boys who were also Washington friends, Mimi Morton, and Ben Torrey whom she married, Peter Wheeler (no relation to my friend Mary), Carol Slocum and her good-looking brother Danny. And then there was Elaine Perry who made the boldest move of all. She married Ted Atkins who lived all the way across the Island in

Town! Some of us were smitten with Tim Hutton, thin, blond and very attractive, who spent his summers sports-fishing. So much so that one year we celebrated his birthday by presenting him with a fish-shaped cake frosted with blue icing.

At first there were no houses across the back road on the Bluff to spoil the view of the Moors and the perfect summer sunsets. Gradually gray shingled cottages appeared on the Long Road to Town that wound past the Sankaty Golf Club and Sesachacha Pond, and slowly crept up the Bluff on the western side of our road. Some landowners built a garage or small out-building, but most who owned land on the other side of Baxter Road considered it precious and kept it wild if they could. In fact, until the 1940's, the stretch of back road from Sunnycliffe to Sankaty Light was the least inhabited section of Sconset. Tourists drove to the Light during the day, or walked the length of the Bluff, but at night the North Bluff was ours. One of my favorite expeditions, shared with my mother, brother, friends, and later husband and children, was to walk up the Bluff after dark, looking in all the lighted windows. Very few houses had curtains so we had a clear view of what all the neighbors were doing — bridge games, dinner parties by candlelight, and inti-mate tête-a-têtes. Sometimes someone would be undressing or brushing her teeth, and we dared not get too close to the house for fear of being caught in the act of peeking! Occasionally we would be discovered by someone sitting quietly on his front porch in the dark, or walking to the Bluff's edge to see moon-light shimmering on the water, but it was a fine adventure. We lived in our own world in Sconset and hardly acknowledged that there was life nine miles away across the Island.

Of course, there was and we would discover the pleasures and delights of Nantucket when we were old enough to drive a car.

# Chapter Fifteen
## The Next Generation

My brother's memories of the period I am writing about are very different. He has the advantage of almost five years, and a different perspective as a male. Thinking back to when he and I spent summers together in Nantucket, I only remember the kind of hero worship that little sisters reserve for their handsome big brothers, and wanting to be included in whatever he did.

As a little boy, Teddy was beautiful with large, brown eyes and thick, dark hair. When he was a baby he was called "Bunny." Early photographs show him in sailor suits, probably bought from Best & Company by one of his doting grandmothers. He was, after all, the first grandchild on both sides of the family and would carry on the family name. After nearly five years of exclusive attention, he had to make way for a baby girl. My father had said that any girl of his would be named Katharine, which might have proven difficult had my parents had more daughters. To avoid confusion with my mother I was always Little Kay (a name I dislike to this day) except to my grandmother Mary Oliver who called me Little Princess.

It's likely that my arrival upset Teddy's easy supremacy, something I was unaware of for years. When I was old enough to understand what a brother was, I was ready to do almost anything for him. That was to work against me, just as it had for my mother.

Norris had played church with Katharine, but since Teddy's goal was to become a doctor, we played hospital, with my beautiful French, felt-faced dolls as patients. I was the nurse, of course. After surgery, my dolls had stitches and red splotches of mercurochrome all over them. I didn't complain because I had been privileged to play with my brother. Less fun, but more helpful to Teddy, was being "allowed" to pack away his tin soldiers at the end of summer, carefully wrapping each one in a

*Edward Garfield Stanley-Brown, aged 7*

piece of toilet paper. He had six or seven regiments, so the job was a long one, but I never felt used, just flattered.

One summer Teddy decided to make a hurdy-gurdy. He was to be the gypsy who provided the music and I, as the monkey, was to hold out a cup and hop up and down. Hopefully, the neighbors would fill it with pennies. At least that's how I remember it. An old photograph, however, tells the real story. Teddy, in shorts and a bandana around his neck and I, in shorts, shirt and sneakers, hold long poles topped with a rectangular box, much like an Oriental litter, with the words "organ-grinder" chalked on the side. On the ground is a stuffed animal attached to a string that Teddy holds. What quirk of mind had me as a dancing monkey?

The Hurdy-Gurdy, Teddy and Kay, 1933

In preparation for an eclipse of the sun in August, 1932, Teddy and his friends built a small and rather crude house in Sunnycliffe's back yard. We had been warned not to look directly at the sun, so the plan was to be inside the shack and to peek through the wooden slats. We were additionally protected because we wore dark glasses and looked at the sun through a pin-prick hole in a piece of cardboard. It was also all right to watch the eclipse through a mirror if you faced backwards from the sun. I was thrilled to join the group on August 31, and, equipped with dark glasses, cardboard and mirror, waited for the magic moment. The *Inquirer & Mirror* reported: "it was a perfect day, except for one white cloud that drifted across the sun producing a curious rainbow effect." The eclipse reached 99 percent totality and inside the shack we were awed by a natural phenomenon of such grandeur.

Teddy sailing with Mamie in 1929

Most of our childhood life on Nantucket was more ordered. Each day offered routines that we simply accepted. Just as the cook had a time schedule, so did we for meals, lessons and chores. We were allowed to eat our breakfast outdoors on the front porch. Afterwards, we made our beds, tidied our rooms and did our jobs. Mine were to water and weed the flower beds, empty waste baskets throughout the house, and to fill the standing, concrete bird bath on the front lawn. Teddy had more manly tasks. He brought in fire wood, laid up the fire and replaced fallen shingles. He also took care of whatever dog spent the summer with us. A walk up or down the Bluff followed, and then we swam on our beach until the ringing of a ship's bell summoned us to lunch at noon.

*Ready to do most anything, Teddy and Kay*

In the afternoon, after I outgrew formal naps, I was encouraged to read for an hour as that's what all the adults did. Only then did the day open up to more carefree possibilities: a trip to Town, swimming at Wauwinet or Dionis, tea at the Yacht Club with grandmother Mary Oliver whom we called Mamie, or playing with friends. Some days the routine varied to include tennis lessons or, for Teddy, tutoring.

Sunday in Sconset had its own invariable pace. Unless the weather was bad, all but Mamie walked a mile downtown to the charming, white clapboard, non-denominational Chapel. There, at age four, I had been christened by Mamie's missionary friend, Dr. Willy Roberts. Grace McKinley played the piano every Sunday, and I was a minor member of the choir which was much more fun than just sitting and listening to a sermon. After church we walked home by way of Mrs. Coffin's house to pick up homemade ice cream for Sunday lunch. It was coffee one week, fresh peach the next, and ginger the third, right on through the summer. Sometimes if the day was very hot, Teddy would make a breakneck race to Mrs. Coffin's and back on his bicycle, hoping the ice cream wouldn't melt on the way.

*Kay—4 yrs. old; filling the bird bath*

Although I don't remember it, Teddy and I must have bickered and argued constantly during our youth. Mostly, I imagine, because I wanted to be included in his activities for which I was five years too young. I'm sure it was a great relief to my mother when Anita Zahn, a disciple of Isadora Duncan, started the Duncan School of Dance in Sconset. At age seven, I spent five days a week there, from nine to six, with little girls my own age. In the morning we danced outdoors on the grass, barefoot and wearing loose-fitting, sleeveless gauze dresses. Under the direction of Anita, Kirsten and Rosemarie, we learned to leap, skip and wave our bodies around to tunes Carol played on the

*Anita Zahn at the Duncan
School of Dance—1935*

flute. All very Grecian and supposedly liberating. The afternoon
was devoted to quiet activities, mainly sewing by hand. It
amazes me now that seven-year-olds would sit patiently for
hours absorbed with needlework. Yet each of us did and at the
end of the summer we proudly wore our creations — flowered
cotton dirndls, white voile blouses with hand-embroidered neck
and cuffs, and elastic headbands decorated with handmade
woolen flowers.

Apparently, my mother reported, I was exhausted from
such long days and begged to stay home, but I only remember
loving it all. In particular, I enjoyed the dancing and was
thrilled to be told after the final performance that I was the best
dancer of the group. Never mind that it was my mother who
said it!

One other memory of my Sconset childhood summers
remains — the clothes that I wore. Mamie lived in East Orange
in the winter and Best & Company was literally next door.
When my mother and I went to visit each spring, Mamie would
plan a "shopping spree" to pick out my summer clothes. As a
result, for years I wore twill shorts with rows of buttons down
each side like sailors' pants, and striped T-shirts in matching
colors. I had sets of them in French blue, yellow, pink, red and
green with white shorts for tennis. An odd thing to recall, I sup-
pose, but I don't think I wore anything else for years.

Each room in Sunnycliffe came to be associated with one
person or one thing. The room off the living room that had
served as Charles Oliver's office was always the Telephone

*"Baby Kay"—2 yrs. old, at
Wauwinet*

Room. As long as I can remember, the southeast-facing second floor room was Mamie's Room, even when it was my parents, and then mine. The room next to Mamie's was an odd one. It had been normally-sized until Lewie added a bathroom for his sister which virtually eliminated half the room. There was just enough space to squeeze in a white iron bed, a bureau and small wooden desk. There was no closet, just a row of wooden pegs attached to the door that led into Mamie's Room for until she died in 1938, she needed a nurse near by at night.

In 1939, this queer L-shaped chamber became Teddy's Room. It suited him well as he was meticulously neat with his clothes and belongings. Without a closet, he stored heavy sweaters and fishing gear in a locked wooden chest, much as Norris did. Teddy hand-lettered a sign for his door which read "Do Not Enter" with a scull and crossbones below, no doubt to keep me out. After he won the role of Stage Manager in the Sconset Casino's production of "Our Town", he thumbtacked the play's posters to his wall which impressed everyone. And one year, another card was tacked to his door announcing the existence of the Ale and Quail Club, a mysterious organization that excluded me. To this day I have no idea how it functioned.

From the moment it was first built it was the Nursery, and it was my room until I was 16. I loved it because I could see all the way down to the Village, what was happening next door at the Dickinsons — who never had shades on their windows — and whoever came up the back road, all from one window. From my other window on the northeast side, I could see the back road most of the way up to Sankaty Light whose beam swept across my room each night. I could also watch Mrs. Mackie playing Solitaire in her glassed-in sun room next door.

The room was next to the bathroom and to the back stairs if the need came to escape. "Oh Kay," my mother would call, hoping that I could come down the front stairs to entertain some visitor's child who had been brought unwillingly to call. As I tiptoed down the back stairs to my bicycle and freedom, I'd hear my mother say, "Oh dear, I guess Kay isn't here right now." I didn't feel the slightest guilt at leaving my mother to cope with her guest and what was probably a sulky child.

At 16, I moved into the Front Room which was the only room without a designated owner. Right away I loved my new home with four windows that looked northeast and out to sea. I too, had my own porch where, armed with my school reading list, I made my way through the required classics. Of those, I remember only *Vanity Fair*, an extraordinarily long book that I didn't much like. An infected foot that immobilized me for almost a week was the only reason I got through it. There wasn't much to do but read. How surprised I was when I read it again 44 years later to discover what a delightful story it is.

I wasn't the only one to use the porch. On vacation, Norris would knock on my door after lunch, tiptoe through my room and settle there in a comfortable chair for his hour of reading, often falling asleep over Trollope or Santayana.

Katharine Stanley-Brown—
3 yrs. old

Although much of my childhood centered around family, Sconset was full of wonderful summer companions. My best friend, Ellen Fezandié, lived south of the Village. Her parents and mine had known each other for years so Ellen and I probably met when we were very small. My memory is that Ellen and I discovered each other at the Casino, where she and I spent most of our early teenage days. Ellen had long honey-blonde hair, clear skin, and huge almond-shaped, watery blue eyes. She moved like a young deer, unhurried and graceful, in contrast to the rest of us who didn't quite have our arms and legs in control. There was something almost mysterious about Ellen that intrigued everyone and fascinated the boys who swarmed around, hoping to win a smile. But to write Ellen off as a languid beauty would be wrong. She was (and still is) intelligent, able, and a fine athlete. We played ping-pong and tennis with and against each other, and my proudest moment was the single occasion that I won the Casino girls' tennis singles match from her. Most years she was the undisputed champion.

One day when Ellen and I were about 13, the manager of the Casino, Louis deBarros, a courtly Spanish gentleman with a waxed moustache and a duckfoot waddle, called us aside. "There's a new little girl in Sconset," he began, "and I want you two to be nice to her. Her name is Mary Wheeler." "Yes, Mr. deBarros," we answered in unison, inwardly dreading any intrusion on our friendship. He introduced us to a thin, rather shy girl dressed all in white. She was almost too clean and dainty to touch, but we grudgingly included her. She was perfectly all right, but not special, we decided.

One night after the movie at the Casino, Mary's father asked Ellen and me if we'd like to come back with Mary for popcorn and fudge that he'd made. We thought that sounded like fun. It was so much fun, in fact, that it became the standard post-movie entertainment for our group that whole summer. Whether or not we were won over by Mr. Wheeler's food, Ellen and I agreed that Mary was a lot more than all right, and by mid-August, the three of us were fast friends, a relationship that has lasted all our lives. Years later, Ellen married my brother's best friend, and I married, Gordon Abbott, a college roommate of my next-door neighbor, Jerry Dickinson. Mary, in turn, married another Harvard roommate, my husband's closest friend and rowing partner, Peter Heller.

# Chapter Sixteen
## Skipping Across Time

Profound changes came with World War II. During the winter in Washington, my mother was a member of the Red Cross Motor Corps. I helped at the Red Cross cafeteria on Saturdays and I was a junior air raid warden, jobs I took seriously. When King George VI and Queen Elizabeth of England visited Washington in 1942, I was thrilled as they reviewed my Girl Scout troop on the White House lawn. Gasoline, sugar and meat were rationed, and we spent a lot of time mixing yellow food coloring with then white oleomargarine to make it look like butter. Like so many English children, Patricia and Paul Jeans were sent to America to live with my cousin Katrina Leeb's family to escape the dangers of the London blitz. But I was young, unknowing and isolated from the real horrors of the war.

Then in February, 1944 my father died. It could be said that he was a war casualty. President Roosevelt had asked him to redesign the city of Augusta, capital of Georgia. It was an exciting project for him — to change a sleepy southern town of dirt roads and nondescript buildings into a proud symbol of southern democracy. He and my mother took the train south to investigate the city's needs and to draw preliminary plans for its reconstruction. But before much progress had been made, he came down with pneumonia and then viral encephalitis. He was taken to the Augusta hospital but the wonder drug penicillin was brand new, in short supply, and being reserved for the Armed Forces. Even if an antibiotic had been available, it might not have helped for had he recovered from pneumonia he might not have survived encephalitis.

As he grew sicker, my mother sent for Teddy and me. I boarded the train in Washington and picked Teddy up in Charlottesville where he was at college at the University of Virginia. Our train was filled with soldiers moving south to boot camps and there were very few seats. My brother was so concerned for my safety that he ordered me to spend the night in the ladies room, which I did, sitting on the floor. We were both scared and apprehensive, and as it turned out, too late to see our father conscious. He died the day after we arrived. His sister Peggy, Teddy and I, and mother made the long, sad journey back to Washington. Although Rudy had always said he wished to have his ashes scattered in Paris on the Seine, that wasn't possible in wartime, so he was buried in the Prospect Hill Cemetery on Nantucket.

I'm not sure that at the time I understood loss and grief, perhaps because as a child I was somewhat removed from my father. In Washington he was always deeply involved with his architectural practice. For relaxation he painted in oil and water color, made etchings and dry points, or played tennis. He and my mother had a very active social life, due in part to his government associations and their many friends in the diplomatic service. They attended benefits, symphony concerts, art gallery openings and embassy parties throughout the winter. And then, in the summers, I was taken to Nantucket. There I was surrounded with women.

It was with time that I came to mourn the loss of a father and to wish I had known him as an adult. There have been times when I looked for his traits in Teddy or me, or wondered if my children inherited any of his talents. I am curious to know how different I might have been had he lived and blessed me with his perspective and light-hearted spirit. But, at 15, I was perhaps less affected and more resilient than either Teddy or my mother.

After Rudy's death, Katharine was emotionally devastated. She spent much of the time in bed, comforted by a stream of friends and the hundreds of letters that arrived. Although she felt very much in limbo, she had difficult choices to make with a house in Washington, and two teenage children to support. Money was short without my father's salary and in the fall of 1944 she rented the Washington house and we moved to New York where my mother took a job reading manuscripts at Harper Brothers, the publishing house where she had worked earlier. Teddy was a medical student at the University of Pennsylvania and I had a last year of secondary school at Brearley. It was a long time before my mother recovered from such a profound personal loss and could enjoy life again.

We still went to Nantucket every summer and, oddly, life there seemed quite normal. There were differences, of course.

We had ration stamps for gasoline and food so the car was used only for essential errands and to meet friends and family at the steamer. As I lived on my bicycle, I was oblivious to what was surely a significant deprivation for my mother. Each evening we walked down to the Chanticleer for dinner. Owned by Mr. and Mrs. Wylie, this charming shingled cottage with its white shutters and rambler roses climbing up its trellised sides was across the street from the Casino. Mr. Wylie himself was the cook and prepared delicious, if simple, food often with meat that our ration stamps wouldn't have allowed us at home. The Chanticleer soon became the social center of Sconset where our friends gathered, not only for food, but for companionship.

Still too young to be drafted for military service, my friends and I continued what, in retrospect, seems like a sybaritic life. One of our favorite activities was roof-climbing. Many summer cottages opened only for August, and in July we picked those to explore. Some of the houses were only two stories high, with oddly-angled roof sections, accessible from a porch. Sometimes we just prowled around, but at other times we found a sunny pocket in which to sun bathe without being seen by passersby or by conscientious caretakers.

When we weren't at the Wheeler's house eating popcorn and fudge, we were at the Dickinsons, next door to Sunnycliffe. There, in the living room, was a player piano of golden oak and behind it, in an alcove, hundreds of music rolls. Jerry Dickinson was the expert and taught us how to pump the pedals just enough to let air come through the little holes of the music roll to activate the keys. Too much pedal and there was nothing but a banging noise underfoot. Some rolls were hard to manage because the melodies were slow. Imitating the sustaining pedal required deft footwork. But with practice we all managed to pump out such favorites as "Alexander's Ragtime Band", "Too Much Mustard", "Pullman Porters on Parade" and "The William Tell Overture."

Freedom came in the summer of 1944 — we got our driving licenses. As I look back, I think my mother was a saint. She allowed me to drive off in the only means of transportation we had for an afternoon at the beach, a tennis game, or other completely self-centered activities. In my defense, I did take over all the marketing and cooking that summer to help my mother who was still profoundly depressed. She really hated anything that related to the kitchen, and I thought it was fun. And the ability now to drive a car opened up the whole Island to me.

The Dickinsons wisely bought an old jalopy for their children, a wonderful tan convertible coupe with a rumble seat.
The car was impervious to mistreatment, sandy or rutted roads,
and it was a great source of pleasure to Jerry and his friends.
We spent happy hours careening over the moors using up what
rationed gas was assigned with an "A" card which allowed the
least available. The moors cover most of the middle of
Nantucket and as early as the 17th century were designated
common lands for grazing sheep and cattle. Dirt roads criss-
cross the landscape, often in such a perplexing way that you
can get completely lost. The area is full of small, freshwater
ponds, stands of pitch pine, rare orchids and heather, blueberries, a hidden forest and includes thousands of acres then unde-
veloped and all in its natural state. Only in the last 20 years
have sharp-eyed builders ferreted out old deeds to parcels of
propperty. Now, unfortunately, unexpected houses dot this once
wild portion of the Island.

"Please, Jerry, the Roller Coaster!" we'd shout and off we'd
go to Altar Rock, the highest point on the Island, where one dirt
road heading towards the Long Road to Town turned into a
series of closely-spaced bumps. Jerry always drove this stretch
fast but in control, and we screamed with both fear and delight
as we jounced up and down in the rumble seat, flying over the
dirt hillocks. When the Japanese finally surrendered on August
7, 1945, we celebrated V-J Day and the end of World War II by
picking up a bewildered but happy sailor in Town, piling six or
seven of us and him into the jalopy and with a large quantity of
beer, heading for the Roller Coaster. At the top of Altar Rock,
we toasted the United States, the Navy, the Army, and the
Marines, our new friend, Nantucket, the end of the war, and
whatever else came to mind. We sang, we shouted, and we celebrated until dawn by which time the sailor, the real hero of the
occasion, was sound asleep in the back of the jalopy.

In the last week of August, 1945, I left to begin my fresh-
man year at Vassar. On the one hand, I was sad to miss Labor
Day with its end-of-summer parties and final Yacht Club Dance.
On the other, my early departure from the Island marked me as
a "college woman", no longer a child but a member of an exclusive club. That carried a distinct panache! Marcia Scott and Babs
Landauer were also headed for Vassar, Ellen left for Wellesley.
Jerry went to Harvard. And Mary traveled the farthest to the
University of Chicago. As our paths diverged we knew we'd
never again share the carefree intimacy of our childhood summers, but we also knew that the friendships we had would
endure forever.

And indeed, the very next summer, most of us were back in Sconset, excited to meet a new summer challenge — the arrival of the Yale Players.

The Casino wanted to revive summer theater after the war and engaged members of the Yale Dramatic Society to perform five plays, twice a week during July and August. Its director, Burt Shevelove, was a vigorous and non-nonsense professional who drove his group hard and expected a perfect delivery, if not an inspired dramatic performance. Marcia, Babs and I thought for the first time that perhaps the theater was our calling. We hovered around the house where the 20, all male, intriguing, unmarried summer actors lived, and offered to help. We painted sets, gathered props, sewed costumes and were occasionally rewarded with small parts in the plays. I was a French maid, Jacqueline, in a drawing room comedy and spent three acts serving pretend martinis to other actors. One time, I rose to great heights and survived. The play's name escapes me but as I recall it was a quasi-comedy based on a Biblical story. I was one of three wives and spent the evening barefoot, clad in a tan burlap sarong. There must have been a jubilant climax to the play for the three husbands rushed front stage and lifted their wives high in the air. As I came back down, so did the burlap sarong, to my waist. Luckily I was wearing a bathing suit under the burlap!

If the season wasn't enormously profitable for the Casino, it was certainly fun for all of us, and particularly for those who enjoyed summer romances with Yale players. I met Jack Leggett, 10 years older than me, devilishly handsome and urbane, and already on his way to being a published writer. That summer we were together whenever we weren't on stage. Being older, a veteran of the Navy and an aspiring novelist, Jack loved talking with my mother and it often occurred to me that he enjoyed her mind more than my company! At the height of our passion we held hands and exchanged chaste kisses under the yellow bug light on the back porch, unaware that we were in full view of my mother and my brother. It was an unforgettable first love. And, in the odd way that life repeats itself, Jack later married Mary Lee Fahnestock, a year behind me at Vassar with whom, at the age of 12, I had played piano duets in Washington. Lee's older sister Clare was a classmate of mine at Potomac School. And when my husband Gordon and I moved into our first house in Manchester, Massachusetts, we discovered that our neighbors, only five houses away, were Jack and Lee Leggett!

The summer we were 18, Marcia and I spent mornings water-skiing off Brant Point, and a lot of time hanging around the Yacht Club to which her family belonged. We had the transparent excuse of being there to arrange lights for some dramatic production, but, of course, we really hoped to crew for the Yacht Club races and be asked to Saturday night dances. The dances were classy affairs. Sun-bronzed ladies in Lily Pulitzer cotton dresses whirled across the dance floor to the music of Harry Marchard, a real band that made our evenings at the Casino with a juke box seem pretty drab. Their partners wore Breton red trousers, navy blazers and neckties from Murray's Toggery, navy blue with tiny white whales swimming across the silk rep. The older men often wore white dinner jackets. Feeling pretty cool, we took our gin and tonics out on the lawn overlooking the harbor and watched the twinkling lights of Town and listened to the waves slap softly against the mahogany sides of the Club's Vineyard class sloops.

The next summer, Yale reappeared in a different and less mature form. A group of college Juniors with time and a bit of money on their hands, rented a rundown house at Surfside on the South Shore, appropriately called "The Shack". Although they are nameless and faceless now, their hospitality sticks in my memory. Every afternoon at five, when they tired of lying on the beach or their legitimate jobs were over, they returned to host a party at The Shack. Marcia and I, through one of the boys who rather fancied her, had a standing invitation to join the group.

We'd make our way across the Island over the bumpy sand roads to the "Fountain of Youth." There on the sagging front porch was a large, galvanized tub full of gin and grapefruit juice, a drink then widely known as the "Sea Breeze." Sometimes a few trays of ice were thrown in, but often the boys just mixed juice and gin with a big wooden spoon and ladled it into paper cups. What gave the mixture its unique quality was food color. One day we might be offered a blue drink, another day orange, another green, and by the end of the week, the whole mess was a dark gray.

Most of us, during those college summers, had graduated from group activity to having our own boy and girl friends. But these were ever-changing relationships and usually short-lived. When a boy you thought was yours for the summer asked your best friend to the dance, it was the end of the world. That is, until an attractive someone else took his place. Hearts were broken easily and as quickly repaired. In retrospect, the summer was pretty frivolous, but perhaps a release and relief from the war years, and an expression of independence. For me, it was the first time I realized that there was life beyond Sconset.

In 1947, the musical revue returned to Sconset. It was conceived as a three-pronged project designed to raise money for the Nantucket Cottage Hospital, provide a community activity for the young, and to bring back theater. The Jerome Cargill Company from New York provided a director, Bill Latta, as well as costumes, the book and a general outline. Everyone wanted to be part of the project, and I felt honored to be chosen as Chairman. Luckily, there were lots of college-aged men and women as well as ex-servicemen taking the summer off who were thrilled to be part of the show.

One morning, as I sipped coffee on Sunnycliffe's front steps, a name for the show came to me — *On the Isle* — with its play on the word *aisle*. The name caught on and a talented song writer, Otis Clements from Baltimore, wrote the title song which was an instant hit then and has been ever since. Jerry Dickinson drove all over Nantucket in the jalopy, decorated to publicize the show. Parents and businessmen bought advertisements for the thick program whose turquoise blue and white cover was designed by artist Paul Webb. Unsuspected talent surfaced from all over and never, I think, have so many people had such fun for a summer as we did that year. The enthusiasm, dedication and sheer sense of enjoyment combined with the pioneer spirit that we were doing something quite new and wonderful made the project unbeatable. Versions of *On the Isle*, produced with the help of the Cargill Company, have reappeared at the Casino at regular intervals since.

*On the Aisle - Isle; curtain call, 1947*

*L to R: Ginny Vaughan; Katharine Stanley-Brown; Elaine Perry; Mimi Morton; E. Allen Smith, President of the Casino; Bill Latta, Director; Jerry Dickinson; Teddy Stanley-Brown; Pete Wheeler*

That same summer, Teddy invited his best friend from medical school to spend the summer with us. Walt Ballinger was not
only tall, handsome and dark-haired with melting blue eyes,
but helpful and polite. And both my mother and Norris were
thrilled that he came from Philadelphia. Needless to say,
Sunnycliffe was a popular place as he and Teddy captivated
many of my friends as well as girls their own age. Each week a
stiff, black cardboard box arrived from Philadelphia containing
fresh eggs, a present from Walter's parents. And weekly, Walter
mailed the box back filled with dirty laundry. Herky Eaton,
who was about Teddy's and Walter's age, also was a regular
evening visitor. He and my mother became close friends
through a mutual interest in music, books and good conversation. He called mother "Effie" and found she was someone with
whom he could share his innermost thoughts. Herky's father, a
retired Army Colonel and his mother, a wonderful, down-to-
earth woman full of wise cracks and wit, were not wholly sympathetic at the time with their youngest son's artistic and esoteric interests. But Katharine, Effie, or more impertinently as
Teddy called her, "The Crow," was wonderfully attuned to
youth, especially those whose interests matched her own. She
was a good listener, open to any topic and objective in her
analyses. Not only Herky but many others sought her advice
about their careers or problems. Young music students asked
her opinions of their talent, misunderstood wives and husbands
contemplating extramarital affairs poured out their anguish,
and would-be writers asked her to critique their work. These
were intellectual challenges that she enjoyed. Her point of view
was liberal and non-judgmental which her followers appreciated. In spite of her Edwardian upbringing, almost nothing
shocked her, nor did she mind when her family referred to her
advice-seekers as "Katharine's Lame Duck Club."

# Chapter Seventeen
# Widening the Circles

Long, carefree summers in Sconset ended with college. There was a new sense of urgency to get on with adult life. For women of my generation, there was the general belief that we would work for a few years before finding "the man", marriage and motherhood. We thought in terms of a job, not a profession or career. There were many exceptions to this unspoken philosophy — women I knew at Vassar who were talented and excited to put their time and energies into the fields of science, the arts and politics. Some, concerned with the tensions of the Cold War, gravitated to Washington in hopes of landing a job with the Central Intelligence Agency or elsewhere in government. Many went on to graduate schools to study law and medicine. New York beckoned with an array of fascinating possibilities and as I loved cooking and writing, I was sure a job was waiting for me at *Gourmet* magazine. As it turned out, I lacked the most basic requirements, typing and shorthand. I spent the next six months in Washington mastering typing, but never conquered shorthand.

In 1950, my mother proposed a trip to Europe, repeating a family tradition. I had no job, there was no war to worry about and so for three and a half months that summer she and I came to appreciate each other as adult traveling companions.

We sailed on the smallest ship of the French Line, the *Flandres*, which soon came to be called the "Flounder" after a turbine broke in mid-Atlantic. The ship was dead in the water for 24 hours but none of her passengers minded. To spend 10 days aboard rather than the scheduled nine meant only added luxury. Hot salt water tubs each morning were followed by café au lait, croissants and a basket of fresh fruit in our cabin. We spent our mornings on deck reading, playing shuffleboard or ping-pong, had our hair washed, swam in the pool or talked with fellow passengers. Our traveling companion was a New Zealand pianist, Dick Farrell, who had been befriended by my father's sister, Peggy Stanley-Brown. In 1945, Peggy, a most generous woman, let my mother live with her in New York and found room as well to include Dick, then a struggling young musician. In 1950, Dick was on his way to a modest concert tour in England and chose to travel with us. He boldly took advantage of the ship's all-inclusive fare to upgrade our wine from the *vin ordinaire* that appeared at each table at lunch and dinner to some rather choice vintages. He also assured us that the chefs were bored with routine cooking and loved to create fancy desserts, and our table groaned nightly with Baked Alaska, crepes Suzette, and pastry shaped like boats or swans, filled with créme Chantilly. While my mother enjoyed the company of a "Colonel King" as he appears in my travel journal, Dick and I found young men and women of our own age. We drank quarts of champagne, danced the Charleston and the Balboa until 3 or 4 in the morning, slept half the day away and were never the worse for wear.

Some of the passengers debarked at Plymouth but we went on to Calais, boarded the boat train and arrived in Paris 11 days after we had left New York. We stayed for a week at the Quai Voltaire, the hotel where my parents had been on their honeymoon. A week later, when we decided to move to the Right Bank, I remember a particularly snooty conciérge who declared: "Mesdames, it is easier to move from the Right Bank to the Left Bank than from the Left Bank to the Right Bank." In spite of this, we had no difficulty finding a charming room overlooking a flower-laden courtyard at the France et Choiseul on the Right Bank. Dick joined us for wonderful evenings in Montmartre, at the Folies Bergéres, and at Les Halles at midnight for onion soup. He also took us to several smoke-filled lesbian and gay bars that we would never have dared to visit by ourselves.

When Dick left for his concert tour, mother and I took the train to Amsterdam, hired a taxi and drove 15 miles north to the ancestral village of Schermerhorn, a rather colorless town dominated by a huge, dark red, brick church. My mother somehow persuaded the church custodian, not only to unlock the doors, but to let her play the organ, a thrill she never forgot. Thirty-nine years later, our oldest daughter, Katrina Schermerhorn Abbott, made a similar trip, but by bus. And in 1991, Gordon and I drove to Schermerhorn to find nothing had changed. It was still a rather dull town, without anyone about. It wasn't hard to see why my ancestors left for the New World!

Back in Paris, we made plans to spend a week in the Loire Valley visiting the châteaux. We would take the train, we agreed, and stay in the charming Hôtel L'Univers in Tours that my mother remembered from 1922. That is, until we discovered the Blue Car. We had just picked up our mail at the American Express office when we saw a light blue Jeep at the curb, sporting a "For Sale" sign. Two attractive, blond men in their twenties lounged against the hood. In a moment of uncharacteristic impetuosity, both my mother and I decided that we needed a car of our own to reach the Loire Valley and the blue Jeep might just be it. "Come," said one of the young men, "we'll give you a demonstration." Suddenly, we were off with them speeding down the *Champs Elysées*, dodging pedestrians, ignoring the blaring horns of taxis and exhilarated with adrenaline! "How much?" my mother asked when we returned. "Three hundred will do," they said. We agreed, signed some papers and congratulated ourselves on striking such a fine bargain. Two days later we went to the garage to pick up the Jeep. I turned the key in the ignition but nothing happened. A mechanic in blue coveralls sauntered over. "*Ne marche pas*," I said. "*Ça va*" he replied. I tried again. Nothing. "*Zut alors*," he shrugged and went back to his job. Out of nowhere a *gendarme* appeared and ordered us to move the Jeep. "*Je ne peut pa*s," I said. He waved to two other mechanics who ambled over and tried to push the stubborn vehicle, but to no avail.

The next day I wrote in my journal: "We went to the garage to look at the car and it was *too* discouraging. The battery was dead and whether they cheated us or what, it was all useless and expensive. Mother exhausted from no sleep." Eventually, she rallied and confronted the garage owner. "You must take this car and sell it for us," she said. " We cannot speak French well enough to make the transaction, but we trust you." The owner smiled and said he would do what he could, but I don't think we ever saw a penny of our money. We parted from the "Blue Horror" with no regrets and took the train to Tours.

The rest of our trip was lovely — full of architecture, theater, good food and delightful friends both in France and in England. My journal provides a picture of heady activity: seeing famous people such as composers Darius Milhaud and George Charpentier in Paris, the artist Salvador Dali and actress Merle Oberon at the Ritz in London, and lunching at the Athenaeum with my mother's good friend, historian Arnold Toynbee. On a more personal level, my oldest friend from school, Anne Commons and her mother joined us for tea in Paris. Marcia Scott and her mother stayed, as we did, at the English Speaking Union in London, and another Vassar classmate, Martha White, visited Windsor Castle with us. I think it took years for me to appreciate this leisurely brush with culture, because the importance of the trip was the recognition of my mother as an adult. It was during this shared experience that I came to understand her, not as an authority figure, but as a friend. And this is a philosophy that has guided me in my relationships with my own children. I try to understand and respect them as individuals and to tear down the barrier between adult and child. I've had wonderful trips with each of them alone during which we have interacted as much as possible as equals.

Mother and I returned to the United States at the end of July on the *De Grasse*, another small French Line steamer. Again, we were 10 days aboard when an accident occured, now apparently in keeping with French line tradition! A deck steward fell or jumped overboard and drowned. With the hope the he might be found, the ship circled the area for 24 hours, but he was never recovered, nor could anyone explain why or how the incident had taken place. As always, there were callous remarks. "Oh dear," I recall one woman said, "I know he plunged overboard because I told him I didn't want any bouillon that morning."

Life aboard an ocean liner demands great fortitude. Consider my journal entry for the first day out of Southampton. The weather was cold and rainy and the small ship pitched and rolled. I wrote: "Felt rather odd but couldn't miss lunch of eggs ravigote, grilled lamb chops, potatoes, cauliflower Polonaise, salad, vin blanc and chocolate eclair. Also tried a Barquette Montmorency (cherry tart)." The days were filled with heated ping pong matches, cocktail parties before lunch and dinner, evenings of soul-searching with the young men aboard, movies, concerts and dancing. The second day out, I met Comte Guy de Talhoüet , a charming young Frenchman whose attentions to me made the trip quite exciting. Later in August, he pursued me to Nantucket, but somehow he didn't seem quite as attractive as he had on the *De Grasse*. What a wonderful introduction to Europe I had that summer! The leisurely entry into an old culture by passenger liner is far nicer than the way we arrive today by air, bleary-eyed, our circadian rhythms disturbed and our senses dulled with jet lag.

Although my mother continued to spend three and a half months at Sunnycliffe, Teddy's and my visits were dictated by our jobs. He graduated from the University of Pennsylvania Medical School, took his internship at Bellevue Hospital in New York and, after service with an Army field hospital just behind the front lines in Korea, he came back a Captain in the Medical

*Gordon Abbott, Jr. in 1950*

*Gordon and Peter Heller, oarsmen, Labor Day, 1962*

*again, in 1969 at Shimmo*

Corps to marry Jeanne Olson, a beautiful dark-haired girl who was both a model and head nurse of the pediatric floor at Physicians and Surgeons Hospital. The wedding was in 1952 and afterwards they set off, as Katharine and Rudy had before them, on a European honeymoon. As time passed, Jeanne came to love Nantucket as much as Teddy does, and they spend their summer vacations there every year. Now retired after a career as a pediatric surgeon and as Assistant Chief of Surgery at St. Luke's Hospital in New York, Teddy has more time for the Island and he and Jeanne occupy their house at Tom Nevers Head for as long as six months each year.

My mother and I lived in New York in the early 1950's and I set out to look for a job. Mary Wheeler was working for *The New Yorker* magazine. Jerry Dickinson was at Columbia medical school, and my best friend at Vassar, Sue Getty, was working at St. James' Church. I still thought I might write for a magazine, if not *Gourmet* then perhaps *Time.* A visit to Roy Larsen proved I wasn't qualified for the latter, but he suggested that I see the personnel director at a non-profit organization that he had started called the National Citizens Commission for the Public Schools. There I found a position as an Editorial Assistant and had a fine time for three years, writing and editing its newsletter.

In 1952, I met one of Jerry Dickinson's Harvard roommates at a crew race on the banks of the Charles River in Cambridge. I was with another of Jerry's roommates, Bob Erskine, and the handsome young man who hardly noticed me was Gordon Abbott. Bob and Gordon had sailed together during college summers, and after the crew race we all drove out to Manchester for dinner with Gordon's parents at their beautiful house overlooking the water. A month later, on Nantucket, Mary and I decided to invite Gordon and Peter Heller, another of Jerry's roommates (he had many as they opened the fire doors between rooms at Lowell House) to Sconset for the Fourth of July. It was a most successful weekend and by that November Gordon and I were engaged. A year later, Mary and Peter announced their engagement as well. Little did I know on the banks of the Charles River, that I would marry Gordon Abbott in 1955, move to Manchester and 31 years later live at Glass Head, the house I had first visited and found so charming in 1952.

Gordon grew up in and with boats and his idea of summer vacation is to cruise the coast of Maine or the Canadian Maritimes which we have done practically every summer since.

As long as my mother was alive I insisted on a yearly visit to Sunnycliffe, particularly after we had children. I wanted them to know the Island I loved, and it was their chance to be with their grandmother. No matter how short our visits, Nantucket became an inseparable part of their lives as well, so a fourth generation came to love Sunnycliffe as much as their ancestors had.

*Nana—Washington, 1959*

My mother, who was by then called Nana by her grandchildren, was fun to be with. She had a lively imagination that children responded to, and told amusing stories Some were made up and some were family anecdotes. She still didn't like the inevitable demands of baby care — those chores were for Jeanne and for me. But she read to her grandchildren, helped them dress their dolls, and delighted in showing a new generation the Hidden Forest and other secrets of the Island. With her they found white heather, saw occasional deer and explored Nantucket's historic sites. She played Gershwin, Cole Porter and Irving Berlin to little Abbotts and Stanley-Browns who leaned against the red upright Steinway, and with the patience that their parents didn't always possess, she taught them to play Parcheesi, Halma and Scrabble.

Nana was a woman of extraordinary and diverse creative talent. Until she was 60 she concentrated on music and writing. In 1961, while spending the winter in Bermuda, she wrote her first and only novel, *Carp Among Minnows*, a sharp look at the interaction of two middle-aged women with a young musician. The plot, embroidered for fictional purposes, was based on the relationship between Nana, her sister-in-law Peggy Stanley-Brown and Dick Farrell, the pianist. Nana's knowledge of the musical field and her insight into human psychology made the book fascinating and unusual, although at the time its frankness shocked some family members. With her dream of having a novel published realized, she turned to another medium, oil-painting, and with surprising success. Her landscapes are accurate in detail and perspective, and evoke the soft air, clear skies and subdued color of Nantucket's beaches and moors. She was thrilled to have her paintings hung in Nantucket galleries, and then, to sell.

*Nana with four Abbotts, 1969; L to R: Katrina Schermerhorn, Alexandra Garfield, Christopher Cunningham, Nana, and Victoria McLane*

Norris died in 1962 and for the next 10 years, Nana presided over Sunnycliffe which adjusted itself to accommodate five Stanley-Browns and six Abbotts. We usually came for a week or two in July bringing, in addition to small children, huge bags of diapers, a play pen, baby carriage and toys. When he couldn't leave work to be with us, Gordon drove us to the evening boat in Woods Hole and saw that we were installed in a stateroom for the three-hour trip. The youngest slept while the others and I had a picnic supper. Soon the whistle blew at Cross Rip, and as we peered out the porthole, if the night was clear we'd see the first faint twinkle of lights. They got brighter and brighter until we made out the dark outline of Town and the illumination of the Unitarian Church up the hill. The whistle blew as we rounded Brant Point, and then came the inevitable jarring bump as we hit the dock. Nana waved, the children shouted and ran off the boat to hug her. Then the nine-mile trip across the Island in the soft, moist night air, the smell of bayberry and pitch pine, the flash of Sankaty Light, and up Baxter Road to Sunnycliffe where Nana had left a blaze of lights to welcome us. The feeling was always the same — we were home again. Once there and settled in, we repeated many of my childhood activities, walking the Bluff to Sankaty, swimming at Wauwinet or Dionis, toasting marshmallows and playing old games. We had beach picnics on the South Shore, trips to the Oldest House and the Whaling Museum, and movies at the Casino. Some years we overlapped with Teddy and Jeanne's family which was great fun for all the cousins. Jeanne and I were busy with our babies and Teddy, whose avocation has always been cooking, provided delicious dinners every night accompanied by choice wines. The children ate earlier and scampered around outdoors in their pajamas catching fireflies or playing "Kick the Can" until they were old enough to go off on their bicycles with their friends. Gordon came every year as well, at least for a few days, and, at times, in our own boat.

*Sunnycliffe's 75th Anniversary, August, 1964; 1st row, L to R: Beth Stanley-Brown, Victoria Abbott, Katrina Abbott, Christopher Abbott, David Stanley-Brown. 2nd row: Jill Stanley-Brown, Katharine Oliver Stanley-Brown. 3rd row: Gordon Abbott, Jr., Katharine Stanley-Brown Abbott, Jeanne Olson Stanley-Brown. Top row: Edward Garfield Stanley-Brown*

1963 was a very special year — Sunnycliffe's 75th anniversary. Both Teddy's and my families were there for the celebration on Saturday, August 3. Eleven of us from the age of one-and-a-half (Victoria Abbott) to 71 (Katharine Powell Schermerhorn Oliver Stanley-Brown) sat down to a magnificent dinner cooked by Teddy and me and served by the much-loved Jessie Fisher. It is recorded in the guest book that we had shrimp cocktail with Russian dressing, roast beef with horseradish sauce, Yorkshire pudding, asparagus hollandaise and several bottles of St. Julien 1959, a delicious red Bordeaux. Dessert was "Gâteau de Chef" with an anniversary message in icing, and champagne. Gordon, then Editor of the *Gloucester Daily Times* made up a special edition of the paper's front page with headlines that read: "World Leaders Send Greetings; Sunnycliffe Celebrates its Diamond Jubilee." We showed colored slides, paraded around the house, and presented Nana with orchids, a beach chair, and a one-foot high pine tree which we planted the next day. When we sold the house 16 years later, the pine tree, growing in a sheltered corner by the kitchen porch, had reached 18 feet and just covered the second story windows.

It was a grand occasion and one that honored a summer house that had brought pleasure to four generations of a single family. There were many more happy moments to come, but never another celebration like the 75th!

*Pine tree we planted in 1964 as it looked in 1977, 13 yrs. later*

# Chapter Eighteen
# Pleasures of the Table

Enjoyment of good food, the pleasure of sharing it with family and friends, and the rituals of fine dining at Sunnycliffe can surely be traced to the family's Dutch ancestry. A well-stocked kitchen and wine cellar were taken for granted by the Schermerhorns as testament to their refined tastes and ample pocketbooks. With staffs of cooks and maids, elaborate meals were prepared with apparent ease. Although Mary Oliver and my mother Katharine cared nothing about the art of cooking, they both appreciated good food. Both Teddy and I inherit our interest in gastronomy from our father who loved to cook, was excellent at it and approached it as an intellectual as well as a gustatorial pleasure.

*Levi Coffin who brought milk*

Until the end of the 19th century the choice of food was dependent upon the seasons. Raw vegetables and fruit were rare and often suspect, and refrigeration was minimal. Mary Henry (Oliver), at 26, described Washington's Birthday luncheon in 1887 in her diary: "A delicious lunch of raw oysters, smelt and dressing, chops, potatoes, jelly and champagne, oyster salad, ice cream and cake with brandied peaches." Her father, Lewis B. Henry, sometimes brought fresh fish out to East Orange from the Fulton Fish Market near the offices of his sugar brokerage, and Homburg grapes arrived from Homer during the late summer. Katharine remembered when she was a little girl in Philadelphia that a fresh pear or a banana was an exciting change from the usual stewed prunes or apricots. And at Christmas, children were thrilled to find an orange at the bottom of their stockings.

When Charles and Mary Oliver first came to Nantucket, they relied on merchants who came to the door. Dave Glidden, grandfather of the owner of today's Glidden's Fish Market in Town, brought fresh fish to the back door of Sunnycliffe. Cod cost a penny and lobster was 15 cents a pound. Island fish was plentiful, and every cook learned quickly how to prepare scup, butter fish, bluefish, mackerel and plaice. Every morning, Mr. Coffin, in his horse-drawn wagon, delivered the milk, and the vegetable man from one of the farms stopped by three times a week. The climate on the Island is ideal for growing produce and Sunnycliffe's table abounded with fresh peas, corn, squash and Mary's favorite, parsnips. In August, when the huckleberries were ripe, an old Nantucketer went from door to door selling his freshly-picked fruit from a galvanized bucket. The ice man came in his truck and Teddy recalls that there was a cardboard dial in the back kitchen window. The arrow could be set at 10, 20 or 50 pounds, whatever the family needed. The ice man sawed off the required amount of ice, lifted it off the sawdust, and, with his huge metal tongs, carried it in to the ice box.

Sunnycliffe's dining room was across from the Telephone Room. Its heavy oval table and caned chairs were painted a bright dark blue to match a ponderous sideboard. Windows on either side of the room gave views of the ocean to the east and the moors to the west. At one side was a small but serviceable fire place. Across from it was a minute pantry with a pass-through window so that the cook could send hot platters through to the waitress who whisked them to the table. A wooden rack ran on either side of a wood beam in the middle of the paneled ceiling which held and displayed Mary's favorite Delft and Meissen plates.

Every morning at eight, Mary presided over breakfast, stationed at the head of the table. She poured coffee from her silver service and tapped the top off her boiled egg with a special gold-plated spoon that didn't tarnish as easily as silver. Bacon and muffins called "Little Gems" were served, and on Sundays there were fishcakes. Occasionally there was French toast and syrup.

Lunch usually featured fried fish, potatoes and a vegetable (often fried parsnip cakes) and cooked fruit. The idea of serving salad was yet to arrive from Europe. Dinner began with creamed soup, followed by meat or poultry, vegetables and a dessert such as pie, cottage pudding or blancmange. But, the most predictable meal was Sunday lunch. Mary always asked the minister who had delivered the sermon at the Chapel to join us, and the menu never varied — roast chicken one Sunday and roast beef the next, with Mrs. Coffin's homemade ice cream for dessert.

The highlight of the summer, as both Teddy and I remember, was a Clam Bake, a glorious affair on a South Shore beach.

Early in the afternoon, a pit was dug in the sand and filled with layers of driftwood for the fire. Lobsters, potatoes, corn on the cob and clams went on top and the whole pit was covered with wet canvas. After hours of anticipation the canvas was taken off, steam poured out, and the food, perfectly cooked, was revealed. As the wind dropped and the stars came out we heaped our paper plates with delicacies and enjoyed the freedom of eating everything with our fingers. Afterwards, when the coals were gray and faces were flaming hot, we toasted marshmallows and sang in varying degrees of harmony.

When Katharine spent mornings on Sconset's main bathing beach with her friends during the 1920's and '30's, they would swim, sun bathe and lunch on a dozen ice-cold clams on the half shell from Mr. Thomas' fish market (he had replaced Mr. Cash) beyond Codfish Park in the Gully.

Another summer treat was a lobster dinner at The Skipper on Steamboat Wharf in Town. It was a grand experience to sit down at a rough wood table on an old coasting schooner, have a bib tied around your neck and be presented with hot boiled lobster. Each of us had a chrome pick and claw crusher, wedges of lemon and drawn butter in a small glass dish. These whose appetites were larger than mine prefaced the lobster with a cup of The Skipper's quahog chowder and steamed clams.

My grandmother enjoyed "taking tea" under an umbrella-covered table on the lawn at the Nantucket Yacht Club while the many-colored sails of the Rainbow fleet fluttered around the inner harbor. She never drank hard liquor but enjoyed sherry and, when traveling, always carried a small silver flask of blackberry cordial to soothe an unsettled stomach. But tea at the Yacht Club was one of her favorite rituals.

The cocktail party as such didn't exist until the 1930's, but Katharine always had a bottle of whiskey on hand (provided by Lewie) so that she could offer her friends a highball. During Prohibition, like thousands of others, Katharine and Rudy tried their hand at making "Bathtub gin" from juniper berries and alcohol with middling success. They were luckier with Cointreau. Christmas came early on December 21, 1933 when Congress presented the nation with the ratification of the 21st Amendment, legalizing once again the sale of alcoholic beverages. From then on the cocktail party was the entertainment of choice for adults at Nantucket. It varied from the big bash with lots to drink and bowls of potato chips and clam dip, nuts and popcorn, to the intimate, let's-sit-down-on-the-terrace-and-sip-our-drinks-quietly kind of affair. Some people had a large party on the same date each year, the Fourth of July or Labor Day, for example. Some included all ages with appropriate food and drink. Others paid back all their social obligations at once with a huge party, bartenders and catered food.

In the 1950's and '60's Katharine went to three or four cocktail parties a week, usually alone because Norris refused to accept hospitality from anyone whom he couldn't repay. Occasionally, he would agree to host a modest party with Katharine and, if they were lucky, Jessie Fisher would make her famous Sconset Sandwiches (recipe on page 148) as well as pass h'ors d'oeuvres and clean up.

Well, of course, life changed, and it's probably a good thing that Mary Oliver didn't live to see the onslaught of shortcut mixes, frozen food and the microwave. She would have hated it all. In the late 1930's, Sconset boasted two markets, the A & P next to the Book Store on Pump Square, and the Sconset Market run by Arlene and Gordon. Arlene's father, John the Barber, owned the garage and adjacent barbershop. He seemed gruff and short-tempered, but he had a kind heart and would solve any car crisis that arose. More than once Katharine called him many miles from Sconset or late at night when her car failed. He never refused to come to her rescue.

In Town, Ashley's Market stood at the head of Main Street, an old-fashioned store stocked with pricey S.S. Pierce products. Every morning a truck from the Bartlett Farm pulled up half way down the street to sell its fresh farm vegetables and flowers. But, as Town became crowded, parking became a daily frustration. Everyone was delighted when, in the 1950's, the First National super market was built just outside of town, with unlimited space for cars. The A & P, meanwhile, established itself on Straight Wharf, and its Sconset branch gave way to Claudette's Catering. The best fish, of course, came from Island fish markets, Holdgate's and Glidden's in Town, right off the fishing boats. There we bought our swordfish, tender Nantucket scallops and quahogs for chowder. Quahog chowder has a flavor and character all its own, a far cry from the bland soup served off Island made from steamers.

In the food world now anything is possible. The availability of foreign ingredients allows us to sample a different cuisine daily from Thai to Tuscan to Cajun. There are too many cookbooks to read and too many food magazines to choose from. But, as a general rule, indigenous food tastes best in its own country. On Nantucket, the scallops, quahogs, blue fish, local corn and blueberries are the best. Nantucket produce stands tall, without apology, in the sea of culinary innovation.

My father made a fine quahog chowder (his recipe appears on page 140). He learned to cook when he studied at the Beaux Arts in Paris, and was understandably fond of all French food. In Washington, he cooked on Sunday nights, often creating a Boeuf Bourguignon or Coq au Vin that recalled his student days. The salads my mother knew were sliced tomatoes with mayonnaise or a pineapple round with cream cheese sitting on a lettuce leaf until Rudy introduced her to a wooden bowl of greens tossed with a vinaigrette dressing. Although he loved French food, when he cooked at Nantucket he experimented with New England cuisine. He would drive to Town early in the morning to buy the freshest fish and just-picked farm vegetables, even as Teddy does now. From him, both Teddy and I learned to appreciate many different kinds of food, and to not be afraid to try something new.

How different he was from Katharine who avoided cooking as much as she could. In 1925, however, she undertook what she considered an enormous task of making orange marmalade. Her letters to Rudy for a week describe the difficulty and then the excitement of preparing the oranges, cooking the jam and finally sealing the jars. With great pride she wrote: "I've made 16 jars so that you'll have excellent marmalade for your breakfast all year, and at a great saving." In 1951, widowed and living in Washington, Katharine took a series of cooking lessons from the Baroness Sounin, an indigent expatriate, and really rather enjoyed displaying her new skills at small dinner parties. Alone she was perfectly happy with an apple, a piece of cheese and a glass of milk. When she felt the need of a more interesting meal, she would cook herself a small steak and boil an artichoke.

If Katharine wasn't interested in cooking, Teddy, at 17, was and in 1940 she turned over the management of Sunnycliffe's kitchen to him. He and the cook Mary Washington were great friends and as Katharine wrote Rudy: "Mary does better for him than for me." Teddy planned the meals, bought the food and arranged parties with skill and enthusiasm. "Today," she wrote Rudy, "he planned my luncheon for eight. We had sherry, delicious clam chowder, tuna fish salad, cottage cheese, tomato sandwiches, iced tea and a custard. Everyone gave him four stars!" Teddy's epicurean tastes developed as he grew. After indifferent food at medical school, Army fare and institutional meals at Bellevue Hospital where he interned, he found that cooking during his summer vacations was a relaxing pleasure. He has his father's flair and, as a surgeon, a concern for precision and presentation. For his wife Jeanne, who cooks all year, it's a welcome respite and rather like going to a good restaurant every night.

In the late 1940's, with the growing informality of our lives, the old kitchen at Sunnycliffe became the dining room. The enamel-topped work table was replaced with a long pine refectory table that had been on the porch. In the back room off the kitchen a washing machine replaced the coal bin as coal was no longer needed for either the Florence stove that used oil, or the new stove that operated with Propane gas. Next to the refrigerator stood a freezer, and to its left was a dishwasher. Sunnycliffe's kitchen had come of age.

The old kitchen was a pleasant and cozy place to eat dinner. Each night, Katharine put fresh candles in the two hurricane lamps with their verdigrised holders that stood on the pine table at either side of a bowl of fresh flowers. Each morning she cleaned the sooted glass with newspaper. Teddy, the Chef, would start his preparations with an early trip to Town for the freshest fish, meat and vegetables. At about five, he was in the kitchen working on whatever meal he had planned. In between watching or helping him Jeanne and I fed, bathed and bedded our assorted children before the great event, dinner. Accompanied by exquisite wines, Teddy's meals were gastronomic masterpieces, to be savored and enjoyed well into the evening along with good conversation. Katharine often said that she would set the table and wash all the dishes for anyone who cooked for her, which is just what she did. Although all of us fended for ourselves at breakfast, Katharine came downstairs first and set the table, or arranged individual painted tin trays to be carried out to the front porch.

My interest in cooking took a different, more homey route. Bread, homemade soup and dishes that just happen from whatever was on hand held my attention. Donn (Donnell) Tilghman, an old friend of Katharine's and Rudy's, spent the summer of 1948 at Sunnycliffe. Donn was a soft-spoken, easy-going but sophisticated gentleman from Maryland's Eastern Shore. Educated as an architect with exquisite taste and keen eye, he found the business of designing houses too demanding. But, like Rudy, he was a Francophile and loved to cook. He was also an excellent artist. Full of enthusiasm but without much money, he opened a restaurant on Nantucket one year which specialized in French Provençal food. He was the chef. It was a short-lived success. But Donn's legacy to me that summer was enormous. He taught me to bake bread, to use leftovers in interesting ways, and how to keep a French soup pot. The old black Florence stove that had been relegated to a warming oven, came back into its own. The pot de feu sat on top and the bread dough, in its crockery bowl, covered with a dish towel, rose gently in its oven.

Every now and then, my mother worried about her figure and went on a diet. One summer, maybe it was 1950 after we had eaten our way through France, Holland and England, she found a new regimen in *Vogue*. I decided to join her in what turned out to be an expensive and unsatisfying experience. For three days we stuck to the spartan menu of black coffee and dry toast for breakfast, and two slices of bread and tuna fish for lunch. I think there might have been carrot and celery sticks and tomato juice thrown in and tea with lemon. For dinner we were rewarded with three ounces of steak and four asparagus spears. But on the fourth day, I found my mother with a box of her favorite chocolate peppermints, enjoying her third! We both agreed cheerfully that the experiment had failed. Better to live with the Greek philosopher Theognes' proverb: "moderation is best in all things", an adage I have always ascribed wrongly to Aristotle.

When we turned the old kitchen into the dining room, the original dining room became The Bar. By 1946 it had the aura of a 1920's speakeasy. The focal point of the room was an upright Steinway piano that Katharine had discovered. Teddy painted it bright red and she was horrified. Instead of chairs, we put mattresses on the floor and piled them high with large pillows. Perhaps it recalled, for my mother, her mother Mary's Turkish Corner in the 1890's living room which can still be seen today in photographs. Between the two high windows that faced south was Rudy's large oil painting of all the fishes indigenous to Nantucket waters. On either side of the painting hung heavy ship's running lights, one green and one red. With only these lights and a standing lamp next to the piano, the room was dim, faintly exotic and, as it was designed to, invited profound and intimate conversation. Opposite the piano stood a three-foot high bar built by Teddy. He added a protective glass top under which was a collage of family photographs. On the front of the bar, Robert Benchley's son Bob, married to our next door neighbor Liz Dickinson, handpainted in rebus form, drinking expressions. "Under the weather" for instance, was depicted by a supine figure lying under an active rain cloud. You could guess "hollow leg" from the single pink leg with a large kidney-shaped hole in it. Night after night groups of Teddy's or my friends would gather around to sing popular show tunes that Katharine played on the piano. Or lie on the mattresses, drinks in hand, settling the fate of the world. I remember one young man whom I hoped would be a beau, gave me brotherly advice one evening. Or perhaps it was medical advice, as he later became a doctor. "Never let a man touch you unless you and he are engaged," he cautioned.

Sunnycliffe was always a versatile and forgiving structure. Rooms could change to fit the needs of most age groups. The glassed-in porch in which Mary Oliver had "taken" lunch was at various times a ping-pong room, a dining room and a painting studio. The back kitchen that once housed deep, slate wash tubs and a coal bin became a modern kitchen. Whether or not he deserves the credit, George Gibson should be applauded for his thoughtful design and vision. He could not have known, from his meeting with Charles Oliver in 1888 what the family would become and need, but he did a fine job of guessing!

# Chapter Nineteen
# Closing the Doors

The sand spit that attracted Charles Oliver in 1888 underwent extraordinary changes over the years that would affect the Island's character but never completely alter it. Geographically, it's the same, a flat evolutionary leftover from the last North American glacier. Many of its moors and rut roads, cobbled streets, shingled cottages and architectural gems remain, in spite of growing development and the rampant commercialism of the modern world.

But, it was the automobile, the airplane and the telephone that were most influential in making Nantucket the popular summer resort it is today. Leading the way in Sconset was Edward Underhill who promoted the village's charms when he built his small housing development. By the 1920s, Sconset was home to artists, writers, musicians and theater folk. And talented craftsmen have found the whole island a congenial and pleasant place to work.

After World War II, Nantucket changed. With reliable air service and car-carrying ferries in operation, summer people flocked to the Island. They brought with them their urban ideas and prepared to turn Nantucket into a fashionable summer colony. Houses bloomed with white wicker furniture and flowered chintz, spouting whale weathervanes, and carved quarterboards with the cottage's name adorned front doors.

Walter Beinecke, whose family invented the Green Stamp, led the renovation of Nantucket's waterfront in the early 1970's. When he first proposed bringing year-round work to local craftsmen by building a complex of studios, shops and galleries adjacent to a modern marina that included restaurants and bars, islanders were appalled. To us in Sconset, the Beineckes were the people who lived in the large shingled house with dark green trim at the corner of the Long Road to Town and Butterfly Lane. All summer, a huge arrangement of wax gladiola filled the picture window on the front of the house. The idea of this family doing over the Nantucket waterfront sounded unreal, but in time the concept was accepted by the Island as inevitable and even worthwhile as every effort was made to utilize indigenous styles of architecture and to preserve the essential and historic character of the town.

As the waterfront changed, so did the spirit of promoting the Island to the tourist. Brochures from the Chamber of Commerce extolled Nantucket's quaint Indian and Quaker heritage, its beautiful beaches with warm water, and its many fine restaurants. Instead of spending four and a half hours on the Nantucket steamer, a faster boat, owned by Hy-Line, brought "day trippers" over from Hyannis in two and a half hours. They bought bayberry candles, beach plum jelly and Nantucket pottery, light gray and decorated with spouting whales. They browsed in art galleries, enjoyed "authentic" quahog chowder, bought postcards and by four p.m. they were gone.

The marinas expanded and by mid-July were filled with large powerboats full of sports fishermen. By contrast, the little Rainbow fleet still raced on Wednesdays and Saturdays in the harbor, and you could rent a cat boat from Captain Tarvis on Steamship Dock for a quiet sail to Coatue and Wauwinet.

By the late 1970's, Nantucket was discovered by college students, many of whom had been impressed with the hippie movement of the 1960's. These latter-day free spirits wore their hair long, slopped about in dirty, tattered blue jeans, and affected the laid-back languor and disregard for others demonstrated by many of their hippie predecessors. But there were real differences — these young men and women had no burning belief in an alternative way of life, they didn't care about saving the environment, and they had enough money of their own to spend the summer on Nantucket. They came in droves, took over the beaches, crowded the bars and worked at whatever jobs they could find.

Those who didn't have family housing rented rooms or houses in Town, often disturbing the peace with rowdy parties and late night noise. Finally, the town fathers passed laws to prohibit more than five unrelated people sharing a house, and requiring shoes in public restaurants. The children in our family weren't goody-goodies, but they did work. One of my son's friends joined the union so he could take a job butchering meat at the First National. My two nieces worked hard as chambermaids at the Moby Dick, a small inn in Sconset, and

Christopher Abbott worked for Captain Tarvis' Boat Rental in Town. My nephew also landed a bartender's job in Town to which he hitchhiked every day.

It didn't take long for Nantucket to realize that it had a numbers problem. There were too many people for the goods and services, too few parking places, too little open space, and too much money. Luckily, a group of concerned, conservation-minded, people stepped up to address the problem. They reasoned that if the public was made aware of the Island's fragile limits, and if development and protection of land were managed together with care, the values that make Nantucket unique could be preserved. Through the efforts of the Nantucket Conservation Foundation, The Trustees of Reservations (my husband was its Director for 18 years) and generous contributions of time, money and property by individuals, much of the Island's landscape has been protected. It will never again be the Little Gray Lady, the Far-Away Island, the sand spit in the Atlantic that it was in its early, innocent days. But then, what can ever remain unchanged?

For Mary Oliver, life was a happy continuum, made possible by the generosity and care her family took to provide for her comfort and happiness. Never did she have to fend for herself. Katharine, whose life changed dramatically after World War II when she became a widow at 52, learned to care for herself. After 22 years of marriage that included cooks, maids and nurses, she adjusted to a very different style of life. And with grace. She got jobs, learned to cook, managed her affairs alone and was still remarkably creative in a number of different mediums.

By the time my generation had children, we did everything ourselves with the possible help of a cleaning lady or baby nurse when we came back from a 10-day maternity stay at the hospital. A different mindset had taken over — a mother was the best person to raise her children. Even if we could afford help, it was a source of pride to go it alone. Dr. Benjamin Spock with his *Common Sense Book of Baby Care*, allayed our fears about parenthood. Babies, he told us, responded to love and reason, and intuition often led the way. To add rice cereal and apple-sauce to a diet of formula before any of one's friends not only showed the world that your baby was superior, but that the mother was extraordinary and through her careful efforts, capable of advancing his growth. And we, the "super moms", set up play groups, did hours of volunteer work for schools, churches and hospitals, drove car pools, cheered Little League games, and then in the evening changed into our long skirts, greeted our husbands, and prepared delicious, gourmet meals. On weekends we played golf, tennis, or sailed, tucked our children into bed and prepared and hosted four-course dinner parties for 12. Some mothers were active in local politics, charities, belonged to bridge or singing groups, had season tickets to the theater, sports and music events. There was no slack in the rope for those with stamina.

As women, we were clear about our roles in life. Having a good marriage, running a household and bringing up children to be successful citizens was fulfilling. We followed our husbands without wishing to be in the lead. They did their jobs at the office and we did our jobs on the home front. No Betty Friedan or Gloria Steinem had come along to suggest that things could (or should be) different. If we thought of careers, in most cases we saw them coming after our children were in high school, able to take care of themselves. The "empty-nest syndrome" hovered as a terrifying time when we would no longer be needed by our children and we would have to find something else to occupy our time. So on we went, whirling dervishes, trying to do everything without quite enough time or help.

Did we stop, as this generation says, to smell the coffee? I think we did at Nantucket. At Sunnycliffe, we loved the wind blowing across the lawn, staring at the endless line of blue Atlantic to the east, lying in a hammock reading, or walking along the Bluff. Spending even a few days at Sunnycliffe had a narcotic affect — you slowed down, earlier problems seemed unimportant and the sounds and smells of the Island lulled you into a mood of relaxed carelessness.

But, it's not the old days, is it? The steamer doesn't sound three times as she passes the Jetties to alert hotels that she'll dock in 15 minutes, so you'd better send the carriages down to the wharf. Captain Silvia isn't on board to blow the steamer's whistle at midnight on New Year's Eve, or give three long blasts when there's a bride aboard. Lots of tourists don't know why some of us toss a penny as the outbound boat passes the end of the Jetty — so that we'll surely return to the Island. And only those who have crossed Nantucket Sound for many years know that you're half way there when the ship turns sharply where the red lightship, Cross Rip, used to be stationed. Those who do remember stand by the port rail straining to see Great Point, or move to starboard to catch the first glimpse of Nantucket Town's gray water tower. No longer do porters stand at the gangplank chanting: "Gordon Folger, Sea Cliff Inn, Ocean

House" and long before that "Point Breeze Hotel." Nor do youngsters get together to shout the once popular farewell to departing friends:

> Paddy-go-whack, go-whack, go-whack!
> Paddy-go-whack, go-whack!
> Wau-wi-net, Wau-wi-net
> Sankaty Light and 'Scon-set!

There are new housing developments across the Island, at Surfside, at Madequet, and at Tom Never's Head in Sconset. And sprinkled through the moors in odd places are new buildings that disturb its natural beauty. Many of the fine old houses are B & B's or fancy restaurants. Catering services provide gourmet, take-out food.

Yet, much is unchanged. Driving across the Island, the eight granite milestones set in place by Peter F. Ewer around 1824, and painted white by 14 generations of his family for the next 100 years, still stand, albeit overgrown with scrub pine and bayberry. And, as you reach the top of Bean Hill, there is Sconset as it always has been, a long line of gray houses against the horizon two miles ahead. When the last bus takes the tourist back to Town before the sun goes down, the Village can be herself. Sconseters still twirl the brass dials and extract their mail from glass-paned boxes in the post office in Pump Square. The Sconset Chapel still opens its doors to many denominations, and tennis players still serve and volley on the red clay courts at the Casino. The Children's Masquerade still takes place in August. And Sankaty Light still throws its beam across the water, in spite of the fact that the Bluff has receded dangerously and threatens the very existence of the lighthouse tower.

*"Plus qui change, plus c'est la même."*

After Nana died in 1972, Teddy and I wrestled, not too successfully, with joint ownership of Sunnycliffe. During those years we spent part of July in Sconset, and Teddy and Jeanne came for August. Dividing and scheduling time equitably was difficult and the same brother-younger sister syndrome that plagued Norris and Katharine recurred. Finally, practicality and expedience won over sentiment and we sold Sunnycliffe. Teddy and Jeanne found a lovely house with heat near Tom Never's Head and spend half the year on the Island. The Abbotts go back sporadically, and each time I do, there's an unmistakable tug at my heart, a nostalgia for what the Island meant to me as a child, and a love of it in spite of all the changes.

What, I often wonder, is the special lure of this flat sand spit? An island, by virtue of its location, possesses its own mystery. It's difficult to reach and those who do, feel they've done something quite unusual. Mary and Charles Oliver must have felt that as they embarked on the greatest adventure of their lives when they first made the trip. Being on an Island requires independence and ingenuity. When the weather is fine it's like any other mainland spot. But a good northeaster, winter ice or a hurricane can isolate an island and leave you to your own resources. So, there's a certain innate excitement and challenge to island living. Before modern transportation made Nantucket accessible, the Island was really special. It was our secret. Only we knew where the Hidden Forest was, where to find the best beach plums for jelly, or how to ride in on a South Shore roller without being "boiled in the surf." Some, like Norris, hated to praise Nantucket for fear too many people would invade what he considered his personal property. When he came by steamer, he made a point of telling fellow travellers about the charms of the Vineyard and urging them to stop there. After all, he'd say, the Vineyard is much more interesting with its dramatic headlands, rocky beaches, tall trees and rolling hills. How he knew I'm not sure, because he was proud of the fact that he'd never set foot on *that* island.

To arrive on the Island is to suddenly shed care and find freedom. The diverse cultures who have shared it would have agreed. American Indians, whaling men, summer folk from the East and Midwest, fishermen, Quakers, Cape Verdeans and theater people all valued independence — the freedom to do what they pleased, believe in the God they chose, and to follow their dreams. I don't think things are very different today, only there are a few more people pursuing their dreams. They come to Nantucket, as they have for centuries, to escape the constrictions of life on the mainland. They put 30 nautical miles between themselves and life's problems which may reflect a "summer resort" mentality, but Nantucket, and particularly Sconset, seem to exude a benevolent acceptance of humankind. It's okay to be yourself and it's okay for me to be myself.

Sunnycliffe still stands on the North Bluff, facing the Atlantic ocean and Spain, 3,000 miles to the east. She served the family who built her well and left an indelible imprint on the minds and hearts of four generations. The way we lived reflected the values of all those who went before us. The house was practical, unostentatious and easy to manage. The lines were good, the construction sound, and she, like those who lived there, knew how to weather a storm. "Don't you worry about the house," our caretaker John Santos said to Nana, "she was built by a ship's carpenter and she'll give with a good blow, just like a boat." Sometimes we need to reminded that a pretty good way to go through life is to give with a good blow.

As the last door closed at Sunnycliffe, so others opened and we've had different, important experiences. Travel to other parts of the world, seeing children leave childhood to follow their dreams, and pursuing our own goals. But a big part of my heart will always be on Nantucket, in Sconset, up Baxter Road on the North Bluff in a summer cottage called Sunnycliffe.

## *END*

# *Appendix*
## *Sunnycliffe's Kitchen*

Lots of good food was cooked and eaten in Sunnycliffe over the years. In the early years meals were simple, hearty and utilized Island produce. Although World War II's shortages were difficult, Americans' exposure to European and Asian cuisine during the war years led the country to a more sophisticated and cosmopolitan approach to food. Boiled dressing on lettuce was replaced with salad greens tossed with vinaigrette. Beef stew became Boeuf Bourguignon, and eventually spaghetti and meatballs were "Pah-sta" with Sauce Bolognese.

Katharine's friend Dolly Caracciolo was an early proponent of yogurt, wheat germ and Blackstrap molasses as nutritionists began to discuss fat, sodium, cholesterol and the dangers of being overweight. Slowly, the country took an interest in organic food as an alternative to highly processed ingredients. Ironically, chemical additives made it possible to enjoy foods out of season and from all over the world at any time of year, thus expanding the country's tastes.

On Nantucket we ate fresh fish all the time, long before doctors warned against red meat. We ate Island vegetables from the Bartlett Farm truck or from the McGlaughlin Farm on the Long Road to Town. We drank Island milk and ate Island fruit. Only after the First National and A & P carried prepackaged produce after World War II did we become familiar with the exotic foods that are commonplace today. Here then, are some of the recipes that came from Sunnycliffe's kitchen over the years.

### CODFISH CAKES
A speciality for Sunday morning breakfast.

  1 pint dried salt cod (Gorton's of Gloucester in a wooden box)
  1 quart boiled, mashed potatoes
  1 egg yolk
  Butter, salt and pepper, crumbs

Simmer salt cod for 10 minutes, then drain. Whip fish and potatoes together until smooth; season with butter, salt and pepper; add well-beaten egg yolk. Form into cakes, roll in crumbs and fry in deep fat until they are a rich brown. [For today's health-conscious, substitute egg white, egg substitute or milk for whole egg, omit crumbs and sauté cakes in a touch of margarine.]

## LITTLE GEMS

Sunnycliffe's cooks used this recipe from Miss Parloa's New Cook Book, published by Estes and Lauriat in Boston in 1888. I know because the page is dog-eared and greasy!

2 cups flour
2 cups milk
l egg
1/2 tsp. salt

Beat egg until light, add milk and salt and beat, gradually, into the flour. Bake for 20 minutes in hot gem pans. Makes 12 cakes. [Another recipe calls for a hissing gem pan which I assume is black cast iron, preheated.]

## ROSE HIP JELLY

Gems were served with homemade jelly or jam. Rosa rugosa grows wild all over Nantucket, and after its bright pink flowers die, the bulbous "hips" turn scarlet. Pick hips when they are soft and remove stems and blossoms. Slit open, cover with water and boil until soft. Rub through a sieve or strain through a jelly bag. For each 21/2 cups of juice, add:

l cup apple juice
l box Sure-Jell pectin
Bring juices to a rolling boil, add:
4 1/2 cups sugar

Stir occasionally. Boil 6 or 7 minutes or until jelly drops from a spoon slowly in thickened sheets. Remove from heat, skim and pour hot into sterilized jelly glasses. Cover with melted paraffin or cap, cool and store in cool place.

## BEACH PLUM JELLY

Beach plums ripen on Nantucket in late August and are found almost everywhere, usually near the rut roads on the moors, and near sand. For Nantucketers, making beach plum jelly is an annual ritual, and no one likes to tell where she finds her berries. Once, a hurricane interrupted my jelly making. Thirty-six hours later when the electricity came back on I finished and the jelly was fine. The last year we owned Sunnycliffe, my daughters and I picked quarts of beach plums, cooked the fruit and bottled the juice in whatever empty bottles we could find for the trip back to Manchester. I didn't make jelly for a week or so, and it came out beautifully.

Pick ripe beach plums and include some green ones for the pectin. Wash the fruit, cover with water, heat to boiling, drain and add boiling water, almost to cover; cook until fruit is soft. Mash and strain through a jelly bag. Measure and add 1 cup of sugar for each cup of juice. Boil to jelly stage, skim off foam and pour into hot, sterilized jelly glasses. Seal and cover.

## CLAM CHOWDER

Bowls of clam chowder, Portuguese bread, chairs on the front lawn in the hot sun, everyone in bathing suits with skin stretched tight from salt water. That's how I remember summer lunches at Sunnycliffe. But, what is real clam chowder? Even the main ingredient is open to discussion. The *Seven Seas Cookbook*, published on the Island, states that Nantucket has three kinds of clams: Clams (or steamers that are really 'off-Island' clams), quahogs and sea clams which, the author states 'have 2 eyes (or muscles) that hold their shells closed . . . the only part worth eating." Some think that clams have the best flavor, but in our family it is the quahog that reigns supreme. The following is my father's recipe.

18 quahogs
8 medium potatoes, sliced thin
2 onions, chopped or sliced thin
8 slices bacon
Flour
Salt and pepper
1 quart milk
1/4 lb. butter, melted

Boil potatoes in salted water until soft; drain. Open clams, separate them from juice (reserve) and cook in a little water until edges curl. Chop firm parts of clams finely. Chop bacon in small pieces and fry with onions until brown. In large saucepan, layer potatoes, bacon, onions and clams. Sprinkle with flour, salt and pepper. Cover with remaining potatoes, sprinkle with flour. Add two cups of boiling water and bring to a boil without stirring. Add milk and bring to a boil again slowly. Add reserved clam juice and melted butter and when hot, serve at once. Pilot biscuits or common crackers go well with it. Serves 8.

This is my brother Teddy's version, quite different, that appears in *Our Whisk for '76*, a little volume published for 'Sconset's Bicentennial. He makes a base that can be frozen and reconstituted when needed.

4 cups fresh quahogs and juice
Good-sized piece of salt pork
4 cups potatoes, peeled
4 cups white onion

Put quahogs and juice into blender and purée. Dice salt pork very fine and try out in large iron skillet. Remove cooked pieces with a skimmer and place in the top of a 4-quart double boiler. Put potatoes and onions through meat grinder separately. Add onions to remaining oil and cook until translucent. Add uncooked potatoes, onions and quahog purée to double boiler and simmer the whole for a couple of hours, stirring occasionally. Freeze, if desired, in 3-cup plastic containers.

To make chowder, put frozen base (or 3 cups unfrozen base) in double boiler and add 1 large can of evaporated milk. Simmer over low heat until base melts and add either 2 cups milk, half and half or light cream, depending upon how rich you want the chowder to be. Using evaporated milk and cooking in a double boiler insures that the chowder won't curdle. Serve in heated chowder bowls with a pat of butter and shake of paprika.

## FISH CHOWDER

Every Christmas my family has fish chowder in the middle of the day. It tastes best when made a day ahead, a boon for the Christmas cook.

4-5 lbs. haddock, cod or scrod, skinned
3 large onions
1/4 lb. salt pork, rind removed
4 or 5 large white onions
1 bottle clam juice
1 large can evaporated milk
4 cups milk
Salt and pepper to taste

Dice salt pork and fry until light brown. Drain and reserve pork bits. Slice onions, add to remaining fat and cook until tender. Slice potatoes; lay on top of onions. Just cover with water and cook over medium heat until potatoes are soft. Add clam juice, evaporated milk and bring to a boil. Turn off heat and add fish, cut into large chunks. Cover and let sit. Chowder can be made to this point, cooled, and refrigerated. When ready to serve, add milk and heat slowly, taking care not to boil. Season to taste. Serve with reserved pork bits and Common crackers.

### COMMON CRACKERS

Common crackers, split in half
Butter

Soak split crackers in water until soft and expanded. Butter carefully and broil until bubbly and brown on top. Serve with chowder.

### DONN'S SOUP POT

In 1948 when Donn Tilghman spent the summer at Sunnycliffe, he kept a soup pot on the back of the black Florence stove, as they do in French farmhouses. The basis of his soup was meat bones and liquid to which he added vegetables from time to time. Everything was simmered in a large, covered enamel pot. Here are Donn's rules for keeping a soup pot:

- Boil down any vegetable or meat water together with bones from beef, lamb, veal, ham or poultry.
- Add celery, carrots, onions and any other vegetables at any time.
- Either keep pot in icebox or simmering on the stove. Bring to a boil once a day.
- Never add starches.
- For change of flavor, add a can of tomato or V-8 juice.
- If soup seems weak, add a sliced onion or another bone.
- Leave bones in pot until all meat has dropped off.
- Skim off fat regularly.
- Season with salt, pepper, dry or fresh herbs at intervals.

At Sunnycliffe all the cooks knew how to fry fish. Delicate butterfish, scup and sole arrived at the table brown and crisp with flour and butter, and snowy white inside. The exceptions were bluefish and swordfish that were broiled and served with lemon wedges. When Teddy presided over the kitchen, his preparation was different. Even today, I use his basic technique, substituting Dijon mustard for the butter and Vermouth.

### TEDDY'S BROILED FISH

Fish fillets (cod, flounder, bluefish, haddock, scrod)
1/2 stick butter or margarine, melted
Juice of 1/2 a lemon
Shot of dry Vermouth
Mayonnaise
Salt, pepper, lemon zest, paprika

Mix butter, lemon juice, mayonnaise and Vermouth together and pour over fish fillets. Let sit 15 minutes or more. Season to taste and broil until fish flakes and topping is bubbly.

Donn Tilghman introduced us to "the casserole" and this one still works well. You can add mushrooms, artichoke hearts, tomatoes, water chestnuts or various herbs to vary the flavor. Sometimes, I recall, Donn started with a layer of uncooked rice that cooked and absorbed all the juices. My mother referred to this dish as "sweep up the icebox for two."

### DONN'S CHICKEN CASSEROLE

1 chicken, cut up for frying
1 1/2 cups sour cream
Flour
1 or 2 large onions, sliced
1/2 cup dry white wine
Uncooked white rice (optional)
Salt and pepper to taste

Put chicken pieces in paper bag with flour, salt and pepper and shake well. If using rice, put in bottom of casserole. Cover with chicken pieces and top with onions. Add wine and sour cream; pour over chicken. Cover and cook at 350F. oven for 1 1/2 hours. Uncover for the last 10 minutes, turning oven up to 400F. to brown top.

Mary Oliver was fond of parsnip cakes. Although I remember disliking them, I have grown to love this vegetable with its sweet, rooty flavor. It's especially good when pureed. Although a recipe for parsnip cakes has eluded me, Miss Parloa provides a good substitute.

### MISS PARLOA'S PARSNIP BALLS

2 cups parsnips, boiled
1 tsp. salt
1 T. cream or milk
2 T. butter

1 egg, beaten
Pepper
Egg and crumbs for dipping

Mash parsnips with butter, salt, pepper and cream or milk.
Stir over medium heat until mixture bubbles, remove from heat,
add the egg and cool. When cold, make into 13 balls the size of
an egg. Dip them in beaten egg and in crumbs. Put in a frying
basket and plunge into boiling fat. Cook until a rich brown. [Ed.
To be parsnip cakes, the balls could be flattened, dipped in flour
(or egg and crumbs) and sautéed in butter.]

Fresh corn from one of Nantucket's farms means summer.
For most of us, freshly shucked ears, boiled for a few minutes in
water or milk, drained, cooled and slathered with butter is the
only way to eat corn. My father loved corn pudding and the
recipe he used came from *One Hundred Recipes*, a collection of
treasures from Nantucket housewives, published by the
Inquirer and Mirror Press in 1927.

### CORN PUDDING
12 ears of green corn "well filled out, but young"
2 crackers, pounded
2 cups milk
3 eggs
2 T. sugar
Salt

Grate corn, or cut off the cob and pound it. Add crackers,
milk, eggs, sugar, salt and bake for 1 to 1 1/2 hours in 350F.
oven. Eat with butter. The Nantucketer who offered this recipe
added: "It is not easy to give a sure rule for corn pudding
because so much depends on the state of the corn. If the corn is
young and very milky, it does not need so much milk. If the
corn is old it does not need as many eggs and perhaps no cracker. Cracker and eggs are put in to stiffen; milk is put in to soft-
en. Old corn will make a stiff pudding. Young corn will make a
soft one. So judgment and experience will be the best guide for
the use of milk, egg and cracker."

After Katharine took cooking lessons from Baroness Sounin,
she enjoyed showing off her new skills. One of her achievements was an omelet, and it turned out well consistently.

## KATHARINE'S OMELET FOR ONE

1 egg
Pinch of flour
1 T. cold water
Paprika
Big pinch of green herbs of choice

Beat egg. In small bowl beat flour with water, add to egg with paprika and beat well. Add herbs. Put a "big lump" of fresh butter into a skillet and heat until steaming but not sizzling. Pour in egg mixture. Keep the flame low and, as the omelet cooks, push its edges towards the center with a narrow spatula. The omelet is done when no more liquid egg remains and surface looks solid. Flip one half over the other and slip off onto a plate.

Donn Tilghman taught me to make the wonderful white bread that he baked for his restaurant, and I've loved baking ever since. The old Florence stove's oven was a wonderful place to let the bread rise.

## DONN'S WHITE BREAD

1 cup water
1 T. lard or Crisco
1 cup milk
6 cups flour
1 generous T. butter
2 T. sugar
1/2 yeast cake dissolved in 1/4 cup warm water

Melt butter. Heat water, butter, lard and sugar in saucepan until butter melts. Add milk. Cool to body temperature, pour into large mixing bowl and add dissolved yeast. Sift and mix in the flour slowly. When dough can be handled, slip onto floured surface and knead for about 10-15 minutes until texture is smooth and springy, no longer sticky. Add flour to board as needed. Return dough to bowl, brush top with melted butter to prevent crust from forming, cover with towel and let rise double or triple its size in warm, draft-free place. When risen, punch down and knead again, reducing dough to its original size. Shape into round ball, cut in half with knife and put each half into a greased loaf pan. Brush tops with melted butter and leave, uncovered, to rise to almost the top of the loaf pan. Bake in 350 F. oven for 40 minutes, or until golden brown crust is formed, and pan, when tapped, sounds hollow. Remove from pans onto a rack to cool. Makes 2 loaves.

My family has eaten quantities of my Cranberry Bread, toasted and dripping with butter. Expedience justifies using canned whole cranberry sauce but the bread is best when the sauce is homemade. Cranberries grow well on Nantucket and were an important crop from 1857 until the beginning of World War II. Before 1959, the 234-acre bog off the Milestone Road was the largest contiguous natural cranberry bog in the world. A complicated network of dikes now cuts it up into smaller units that deprives the bog of its unique status. In 1968, to preserve the bog, the Nantucket Conservation Foundation took over the assets of Nantucket Cranberries, and in 1980 purchased the man-made Windswept Cranberry Bog for a total of 1,205 acres, 40 of which are cultivated at present. Nantucket cranberries are sold to Ocean Spray Cranberry Inc. in Middleboro, Massachusetts, which provides us with much of the commercial cranberry juice and sauce that we buy.

## CRANBERRY BREAD

2 cups flour, sifted
3/4 cup sugar
1/2 tsp. baking soda
1/2 tsp. salt
1 tsp. cinnamon
1 large egg
1 large can whole cranberry sauce (or 2 cups homemade)

Grease and flour a loaf pan. Sift flour and dry ingredients together in a large bowl. Drop in egg and cranberry sauce; mix thoroughly. Bake at 350 F. for 1 to 1 1/2 hours or until cake tester in middle of loaf comes out clean. Makes 1 loaf. This bread freezes beautifully.

In the 1940s we ate salad every night, with the Baroness Sounin's vinaigrette dressing.

## FRENCH DRESSING

3 T. olive oil
1 clove garlic, minced
1 1/2 tsp. herb wine vinegar
1 demitasse cup herbs (1/3 dry herbs to 2/3 fresh herbs)
   thyme, chives, basil, marjoram, tarragon, sorrel, parsley

Marinate minced garlic in oil, add vinegar, herbs and toss with greens.

When salad was the main course it was Chef's, Niçoise, my Chicken, Lobster for special occasions or Teddy's Crab Louis (which he is the first to say is not from Nantucket at all, but a specialty of the Palace Hotel in San Francisco). Still, he made it often at Sunnycliffe.

### TEDDY'S CRAB LOUIS

6 oz. fresh crabmeat
Bibb lettuce
Hardboiled egg quarters
Black olives
Marinated artichoke hearts

### LOUIS DRESSING

Mayonnaise
Chili sauce
Lemon juice
Rice wine vinegar
Salt and black pepper
Worcestershire sauce
Dried chives
Ketchup
Dijon or Coleman's dry mustard

Whisk sauce ingredients together, using proportions to taste. Arrange crab meat on lettuce, and decorate with egg quarters, olives and artichoke hearts. Serves 2.

### QUICK NIÇOISE SALAD

1 large can water-packed tuna fish
1 can cooked white potatoes
1 green pepper, sliced
1 can flat anchovies, drained
2-3 tomatoes, diced
1 can whole green beans
1 can medium pitted black olives
1 small red onion, sliced
2 hardboiled eggs (optional)
Vinaigrette dressing

Break up tuna fish in serving bowl. Dice potatoes and add with beans, olives, green pepper, onion, anchovies, tomatoes and eggs. Toss with dressing and serve to 4.

### MY CHICKEN SALAD

4 whole chicken breasts, boned
2 large tomatoes
Mayonnaise (not sweet kind)
2 T. fresh tarragon or 1 heaping tsp. dry
2 pkgs. frozen chopped spinach, thawed and drained
1/4 cup pine nuts, toasted
Fresh lemon juice
1 T. Dijon mustard
1/2 tsp. cumin powder

Steam chicken breasts until cooked through, about 25 minutes. Cool and tear into bite-sized pieces. Dice tomatoes. Combine chicken, spinach, tomatoes and pine nuts in salad bowl and add mayonnaise, tarragon, lemon juice, mustard and cumin. Toss well. Salt and pepper to taste. If possible, chill for 3 or 4 hours. Makes 4 servings.

For years, everyone in Sconset loved Jessie Fisher's "sandwiches" that appeared at cocktail parties. And for good reason; they're addictive!

### JESSIE'S SCONSET SANDWICHES

Bermuda onions
White vinegar
Mayonnaise
Sugar
Gulden's brown mustard
1-inch bread rounds

Soak thinly sliced onions in ice water with a good shot of vinegar added, for at least 1/2 hour. Drain and pat dry. Mix together mayonnaise, mustard and sugar to taste. Just before serving, spread sauce on one side of bread round and cover with onion slice. You can add an extra dollop of sauce on top if you want. As Teddy says "people inhale them."

### SCONSET PÂTÉ

Katharine served this at all her Sunnycliffe cocktail parties so it became known as Nana's pâté, whether or not she invented it.

1 3 oz. pkg. cream cheese, softened
1 small can Sell's liver paste
1/2 T. unflavored gelatin
1 can consommé
1 1/2 jiggers best brandy

Start this a day before using. Mix cream cheese and liver paste together, pour over brandy and marinate overnight in refrigerator. Next day, dissolve gelatin in consommé over low heat. Pour enough into 1-pint mold or bowl to cover bottom; chill for an hour. Place cheese mixture in center of mold and pour over rest of consommé. Let set for at least 3 hours. Turn out and serve with any unsalted crackers.

When Christopher Abbott was about 12, he invented this for a Sunnycliffe party. For a surprise, we had a caterer recreate it for him 21 years later at the rehearsal dinner before his wedding in Sconset in 1989!

## CHRIS' DIP

1 cup sour cream
1 cup cottage cheese, drained
1 pkg. Good Seasons Italian salad dressing mix
Fresh chives, parsley and tarragon, all chopped fine

Mix all ingredients together and chill for at least 2 hours to blend flavors. Before serving, sprinkle top with paprika and garnish with parsley and more chives. Serve with crackers or chips.

During the 1930s, strange and often sweet cocktails emerged. I can remember my father mixed pomegranate juice with gin for what looked like a beautiful drink, however odd it may have tasted. My mother was fond of Manhattans, a mixture of Rye whiskey and sweet Vermouth. Among her recipes, I found a torn sheet of paper that recalls the parties Lewie hosted at Shimmo.

## SHIMMO COCKTAILS FOR SIX

3/4 glass of apple jack
1 tsp. powdered sugar
1/2 glass Bacardi rum
1 tsp. maple syrup
1 can grapefruit juice (10-12 oz.)
Shake all together with ice.
or
1/2 glass gin
1/2 glass Bacardi rum
1 tsp. sugar
1 can grapefruit juice
Grenadine for color
Shake all together with ice.

Berries grow well on Nantucket, particularly cranberries, elderberries and blueberries. Many old recipes call for huckleberries, interchangeable with blueberries, but, in fact, the two berries have different origins. In case you've always wanted to know, the blueberry is the edible berry of several North American shrubs of the genus *Vaccinium* while the huckleberry, though related, is the fruit of genus *Gaylussacia* , perhaps a variant of the whortleberry. Now that the distinction has been made, you can try the following with either berry!

### MARIE'S HUCKLEBERRY PUDDING
1/4 cup butter
1/2 cup sugar
1/2 cup milk
1 tsp. baking powder
Pinch of salt
1 cup huckleberries
1 egg

### SAUCE
2 tsp. butter
1 tsp. flour
1/2 cup sugar
1 cup boiling water
1 cup huckleberries

Cream together butter and sugar, add milk, egg and dry ingredients sifted together. Carefully fold in berries. Pour into shallow buttered pan and bake at 300 F. 1/2 an hour, or until done. For sauce, combine all ingredients and cook until berries burst and color the sauce. Serve hot.

My father liked to make Indian Pudding out of the *Nantucket Cook Book*.

### BAKED INDIAN PUDDING
2 quarts milk
2 cup molasses
2 cups corn meal
2 or 3 eggs (optional)

Boil the milk and scald the meal with it, mixing gradually and thoroughly. Sweeten with molasses and mix in eggs. Bake in a shallow buttered dish for 2-3 hours at 325 F.

With Mary Washington in the kitchen we devoured her cakes, homemade doughnuts and luscious pies. Later, when we had a freezer, Katharine kept half gallons of ice cream; vanilla, coffee and her favorite, Frozen Pudding. Her idea of a fine and certainly quick dessert was vanilla ice cream with Hershey's chocolate syrup heated and poured over it. Sometimes I baked cookies, especially after my four children arrived, but usually we opened up the top of the old Florence stove to grab whatever store-bought kind was around. Dessert was more apt to be cut up fresh peaches, blueberries or melon. Katharine always kept a box of chocolate peppermints on hand for those who needed a jolt of sugar.

In 1948 my friend Mary's mother gave me her recipe for coffee cake. I loved the name.

### SNICKERDOODLES

1 cup sugar
1/2 cup butter
1 egg
2 1/2 cups flour
1/2 tsp. salt
2 tsp. baking powder
1 cup milk
1/2 cup nuts, dredged with flour
Cinnamon sugar

Cream sugar and butter until light and fluffy. Mix in egg. Sift together salt, baking powder and flour, and add alternately with milk. Fold in nuts. Put into 2 square greased pans and sprinkle with cinnamon sugar. Bake for 20 minutes at 375 F. Cut into squares when cool.

In my files, I came across one last recipe for what sounds like a meringue, but who is Mary? The cook, Mary Washington? My grandmother, Mary Oliver? Mary Hovan, a one-time baby nurse? Mary Dickinson Herbert, our next door neighbor? Or Mary Wheeler Heller, my friend? Thanks to her, whoever she is, for the recipe.

### MARY'S COOKIES

1 cup walnuts, rolled but not too fine
2 egg whites
Pinch of salt
Dash of almond extract

Beat egg whites and salt until they hold their shape. Gradually, beat in sugar, a tablespoon at a time, until mixture is

stiff, but not dry. Beat in almond extract. Fold in walnuts.
Spread by teaspoonfuls on greased baking sheet and bake at 250
F. until firm and dry, not brown. Makes 18 cookies.

# HENRY

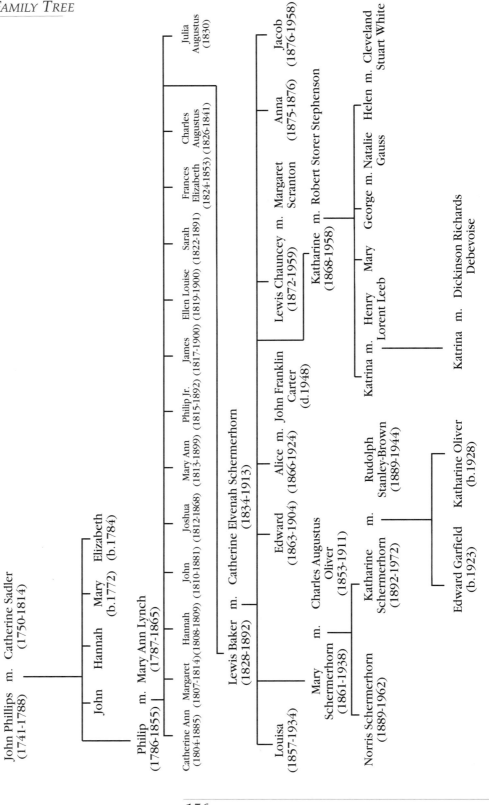

# OLIVER

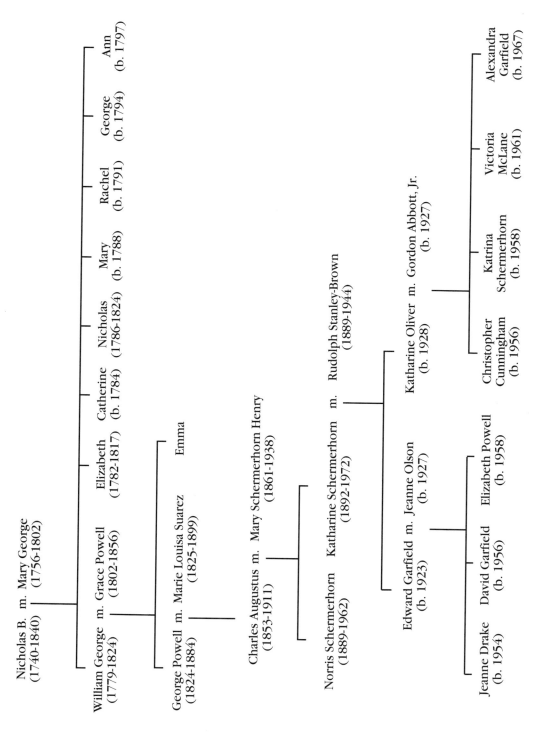

Nicholas B.  m.  Mary George
(1740-1840)       (1756-1802)

Elizabeth        Catherine        Nicholas        Mary        Rachel        George        Ann
(1782-1817)      (b. 1784)       (1786-1824)     (b. 1788)   (b. 1791)    (b. 1794)   (b. 1797)

William George  m.  Grace Powell
(1779-1824)         (1802-1856)

Emma

George Powell  m.  Marie Louisa Suarez
(1824-1884)         (1825-1899)

Charles Augustus  m.  Mary Schermerhorn Henry
(1853-1911)            (1861-1938)

Norris Schermerhorn    Katharine Schermerhorn    m.    Rudolph Stanley-Brown
(1889-1962)            (1892-1972)                      (1889-1944)

Katharine Oliver  m.  Gordon Abbott, Jr.
(b. 1928)             (b. 1927)

Edward Garfield  m.  Jeanne Olson
(b. 1923)            (b. 1927)

Christopher        Katrina        Victoria        Alexandra
Cunningham         Schermerhorn   McLane          Garfield
(b. 1956)          (b. 1958)      (b. 1961)       (b. 1967)

Jeanne Drake    David Garfield    Elizabeth Powell
(b. 1954)       (b. 1956)         (b. 1958)

# Bibliography

*A Casino Album 1899—1974*. Heller, Mary Wheeler. Siasconset Casino Association, Nantucket, 1974.

*A Few Trips to Parnassus*. Unpublished autobiography. Stanley-Brown, Katharine. 1972.

Diaries of Mary Schermerhorn Henry, 1884—1888.

*The Island Steamers*. Morris, Paul G. and Joseph F. Morin. Nantucket Nautical Publishers, 1977.

Letters between Katharine Oliver Stanley-Brown and Rudolph Stanley-Brown, 1923—1943.

*Nantucket, The Life of an Island*. Hoyt, Edwin P. Steven Green Press, Brattleboro, VT., 1978.

*Nantucket's Shipwrecks and Railroad*. *Inquirer and Mirror* reprint. Nantucket.

*Old Nantucket, The Faraway Island*. Stevens, Williams O. Dodd, Mead & Co., New York, 1936.

*'Sconset Heydey*. Barnes, Margaret Fawcett. Inquirer and Mirror, 1979.

*'Sconset Memories*. Stanley-Brown, Edward G. Historic Nantucket, Vol. 32, No. 4. 1985.

*Splendor Sailed the Sound*. Foster, George H. and Peter C. Weiglin. Mid-State Associates and Potential Group, Inc., 1989

# *About the Author*

Like three generations of her family before her, Katharine Stanley-Brown Abbott spent her summers at Sunnycliffe, the cottage on Nantucket that her grandfather had built in 1887. A Vassar graduate, she is a freelance writer for newspapers, magazines and newsletters and the co-editor of two cookbooks, *Essex County Cooks* and *More Essex County Cooks*. Active as a board member of many charitable organizations, she has served as President of the Beverly Hospital Aid Association, Chairman of the Harvard Food Services Visiting Committee, Trustee and Chairman of the Board of Trustees at Brookwood School, and Chairman of the Independent School Chairman's Association. She is the mother of four children. Her interests include outdoor sports, particularly tennis and skiing, reading, cooking and a wide range of crafts. She lives with her husband in Manchester, Massachusetts.